First World War
and Army of Occupation
War Diary
France, Belgium and Germany

58 DIVISION
174 Infantry Brigade
London Regiment
6th (City of London) Battalion (Rifles)
1 February 1918 - 28 February 1919

WO95/3005/3

The Naval & Military Press Ltd
www.nmarchive.com
Published in association with The National Archives

Published by

The Naval & Military Press Ltd

Unit 10 Ridgewood Industrial Park,

Uckfield, East Sussex,

TN22 5QE England

Tel: +44 (0) 1825 749494

www.naval-military-press.com

www.nmarchive.com

This diary has been reprinted in facsimile from the original. Any imperfections are inevitably reproduced and the quality may fall short of modern type and cartographic standards.

© Crown Copyright
Images reproduced by permission of The National Archives, London, England, 2015.

Contents

Document type	Place/Title	Date From	Date To
Heading	WO95/3005/3		
Heading	58 Division 174 Bde 1/6 London Regt 1918 Feb-1919 Feb From 47 Div-140 Bde To 2 Div 2 Light Bde		
Heading	War Diary Of 2/7th London Regt Vol 192		
War Diary	Demuin	01/02/1918	08/02/1918
War Diary	Chauny	08/02/1918	08/02/1918
War Diary	Line	09/02/1918	28/02/1918
War Diary	Pierremande	28/02/1918	28/02/1918
Operation(al) Order(s)	Operation Order No.1 6th Bn London Regiment	07/02/1918	07/02/1918
Operation(al) Order(s)	Order No.2 6th Bn London Regiment	08/02/1918	08/02/1918
Operation(al) Order(s)	Operation Order No.3 6th Bn London Regiment	27/02/1918	27/02/1918
War Diary	Erremande	01/03/1918	01/03/1918
War Diary	Battle Zone	20/03/1918	21/03/1918
War Diary	Paul Au Bois	26/03/1918	30/03/1918
Heading	174th Inf. Bde 58th Div War Diary 6th Battn. The London Regiment April 1918		
War Diary	Near Bainsin	01/04/1918	02/04/1918
War Diary	Villers Bretonneux	02/04/1918	05/04/1918
War Diary	Boves	06/04/1918	11/04/1918
War Diary	Villers Bretonneux	13/04/1918	17/04/1918
War Diary	Boves	17/04/1918	17/04/1918
War Diary	Boutillerie	19/04/1918	25/04/1918
War Diary	Bellancourt	26/04/1918	30/04/1918
Heading	Appendices A A.1 B C D E F		
Miscellaneous	Operation Order P.4 By Major W.F. Whitehead D.S.O.		
Operation(al) Order(s)	6th Bn London Regt. Operation Order P.5	02/04/1918	02/04/1918
Miscellaneous	Narrative Of Events Of 6th Bn. London Regiment	09/04/1918	09/04/1918
Miscellaneous	My Dear Colonel	06/04/1918	06/04/1918
Operation(al) Order(s)	6th Bn. The London Regiment Order No. P.7	09/04/1918	09/04/1918
Operation(al) Order(s)	6th Bn London Regt. Operation Order No.P. 8	13/04/1918	13/04/1918
Operation(al) Order(s)	6th Bn London Regiment Operation Order No.18	26/04/1918	26/04/1918
War Diary	Bellancourt	01/05/1918	05/05/1918
War Diary	Mirvaux	06/05/1918	10/05/1918
War Diary	Warloy	11/05/1918	31/05/1918
Operation(al) Order(s)	Operation Order No.12	17/05/1918	17/05/1918
Operation(al) Order(s)	Order No.14 6th Bn. The London Regt.	10/05/1918	10/05/1918
Operation(al) Order(s)	6th Bn. London Regt Operation Order No.15	18/05/1918	18/05/1918
Miscellaneous	March Table To Accompany 17th Inf. Brigade Order No.18		
Miscellaneous	B Form Messages And Signals		
Miscellaneous	Note		
War Diary	Warloy	01/06/1918	04/06/1918
War Diary	Daily Mail Woods Contay	04/06/1918	09/06/1918
War Diary	Fourdrinroy	10/06/1918	16/06/1918
War Diary	Lavieville	17/06/1918	17/06/1918
War Diary	Lavieville East Of	18/06/1918	22/06/1918
War Diary	Lavieville Defence Line	24/06/1918	30/06/1918
Operation(al) Order(s)	6th Bn. London Regiment Operation Order No.20	05/06/1918	05/06/1918
Operation(al) Order(s)	6th Bn. London Regiment Operation Order No.21	10/06/1918	10/06/1918
Operation(al) Order(s)	6th Bn. London Regiment Operation Order No.23	16/06/1918	16/06/1918

Type	Description	Start	End
Operation(al) Order(s)	6th Bn. London Regiment Operation Order No.24	17/06/1918	17/06/1918
Operation(al) Order(s)	6th Bn. London Regiment Operation Order No.25	18/06/1918	18/06/1918
Operation(al) Order(s)	6th Bn. London Regiment Operation Order No.26	24/06/1918	24/06/1918
Operation(al) Order(s)	6th Battalion London Regiment Operation Order No.27	26/06/1918	26/06/1918
Operation(al) Order(s)	6th Bn London Regiment Operation Order No.28	28/06/1918	28/06/1918
Operation(al) Order(s)	6th Bn London Regiment Operation Order No.28/1	28/06/1918	28/06/1918
Miscellaneous	6th Bn London Regiment Warning Order No.29	29/06/1918	29/06/1918
War Diary	Albert S.W Of	01/07/1918	31/07/1918
Operation(al) Order(s)	Operation Order No.30 6th Bn. London Regiment	03/07/1918	03/07/1918
Operation(al) Order(s)	6th Bn. London Regiment Operation Order No.31	05/07/1918	05/07/1918
Operation(al) Order(s)	Operation Order No.31 6th Bn. London Regiment	07/07/1918	07/07/1918
Operation(al) Order(s)	6th Bn London Regiment Operation Order No.32		
Operation(al) Order(s)	6th Bn London Regiment Operation Order No.33	09/07/1918	09/07/1918
Miscellaneous	6th Bn London Regiment Warning Order No.34	11/07/1918	11/07/1918
Operation(al) Order(s)	6th Bn. London Regiment Operation Order No.34	12/07/1918	12/07/1918
Miscellaneous	6th Bn. London Regiment Warning Order No.36		
Operation(al) Order(s)	6th Bn. London Regiment Operation Order No.36	18/07/1918	18/07/1918
Operation(al) Order(s)	6th Bn. London Regiment Operation Order No.37	23/07/1918	23/07/1918
Miscellaneous	Addenda No.1 To Operation Order No.37	23/07/1918	23/07/1918
Operation(al) Order(s)	6th Bn. London Regiment Operation Order No.37a	23/07/1918	23/07/1918
Miscellaneous	6th Bn. London Regiment Warning Order No.38	26/07/1918	26/07/1918
Operation(al) Order(s)	6th Bn. London Regiment Operation Order No.39	26/07/1918	26/07/1918
Miscellaneous	6th Bn. London Regiment Addenda No.1 To Operation Order No.39	27/07/1918	27/07/1918
Miscellaneous	A Form Messages And Signals		
Heading	174th Bde 58th Div 6th Battalion London Regiment August 1918		
War Diary	Maps Sheet 62D.N.E. 62.C.N.W. Round Wood Near Contay	01/08/1918	01/08/1918
War Diary	Canaples	02/08/1918	03/08/1918
War Diary	Lahoussoye	04/08/1918	13/08/1918
War Diary	Round Wood Near Contay	13/08/1918	21/08/1918
War Diary	Heilly	22/08/1918	31/08/1918
Operation(al) Order(s)	6th Bn. London Regiment Operation Order No.41	01/08/1918	01/08/1918
Miscellaneous	6th Bn. London Regiment Warning Order No.41	04/08/1918	04/08/1918
Miscellaneous	Report On Operations 6th Bn. London Regiment	09/08/1918	09/08/1918
Miscellaneous	Remarks	15/08/1918	15/08/1918
Operation(al) Order(s)	6th Bn London Regiment Operation Order No.5	21/08/1918	21/08/1918
Miscellaneous	Narrative Of Operations On The 26th, 27th And 28th August 1918	28/08/1918	28/08/1918
Miscellaneous	Narrative Of Operation Of The 31st August 1918	04/09/1918	04/09/1918
War Diary		01/09/1918	25/09/1918
War Diary	Ref Sheet Lens II	26/09/1918	30/09/1918
Operation(al) Order(s)	Operation Order No.123 6th Bn. London Regt	06/09/1918	06/09/1918
Miscellaneous	Summary Of Operations September 8th, 9th 10th 1918	11/09/1918	11/09/1918
Operation(al) Order(s)	Operation Order No.124 6th Bn. London Regiment	25/09/1918	25/09/1918
Operation(al) Order(s)	Operation Order No.125 6th Bn. London Regiment	29/09/1918	29/09/1918
War Diary	Le Brebis Lens N.W. Of	01/10/1918	08/10/1918
War Diary	Bois De Riaumont	08/10/1918	11/10/1918
War Diary	Canal De La Haute	12/10/1918	14/10/1918
War Diary	Courrieres	15/10/1918	20/10/1918
War Diary	Nomain	21/10/1918	26/10/1918
War Diary	Rongy	27/10/1918	07/11/1918
War Diary	Blehaires	08/11/1918	08/11/1918
War Diary	Rocourt	09/11/1918	09/11/1918
War Diary	Beloiel	10/11/1918	11/11/1918

War Diary	Grosage	11/11/1918	16/11/1918
War Diary	Peruwelz	17/11/1918	27/02/1919
War Diary	Roucourt	27/02/1919	28/02/1919
Heading	58 Division 174 Bde 2/6 Bn London Regt 1915 Sept-1916 Feb 1917 Jan-1918 Jan Absorbed By 1/6 Bn 1916 Feb		

WO 95/3005/3

58 DIVISION
174 BDE

1/6 LONDON REGT

1918 FEB — 1919 FEB

FROM 47 DIV - 140 BDE

ABSORBED 2/6 BN FEB 18

TO 2 DIV 2 LIGHT BDE

174/58.

WO/172

WAR DIARY
OF
2/4th LONDON REGT.

WAR DIARY
or
INTELLIGENCE SUMMARY.
(Erase heading not required.)

Army Form C. 2118.

Place	Date	Hour	Summary of Events and Information	Remarks and references to Appendices
DEMUIN	1st Feb. 1918		1/6th Battalion London Regt and 2/6th Battalion London Regt amalgamated dated 31/1/18. Lieut. Col. C.B. Benson D.S.O. appointed Commanding Officer and Major J.H. Kelly M.C. appointed 2nd in Command. Major Whitehead D.S.O. appointed 2nd in Command of 7th Battalion London Regt.	msg
DEMUIN	2		8 Officers and 196 O.R. joined from 1/6th Battalion London Regiment. Major J.H. Kelly M.C. assumes temporary command of the 6th Battalion London Regt in the absence of Lieut. Col. C.B. Benson D.S.O. (on leave).	msg
DEMUIN	3-5		Training and reorganisation	
DEMUIN	5th		Lieut. Col. C.B. Benson D.S.O. returned from leave and assumed command of the battalion.	msg
DEMUIN	5-8		Training	
DEMUIN - CHAUNY	8th		The battalion moved to CHAUNY by march route to VILLERS-BRETONNEUX thence by train to APPILLY thence by lorries to CHAUNY.	APPENDIX A msg
LINE	9th		The battalion relieved 16th Battalion Manchester Regt in the line. Details, 2 M Stores and transport remained at CHAUNY.	APPENDIX B msg
LINE	9-18		Holding the line.	msg
LINE	18th		1 O.R. casualty - wounded.	msg
LINE	18-26		Holding the line.	msg

WAR DIARY
or
INTELLIGENCE SUMMARY.
(Erase heading not required.)

Army Form C. 2118.

Place	Date	Hour	Summary of Events and Information	Remarks and references to Appendices
LINE	24th	—	2.M. Stores and Transport-Limbers moved to AUTREVILLE.	msg
LINE	25th	—	13 Officers and 53 O.R. reinforcements reported to unit. 13 officers joined unit in the line and 53 O.R. remained at Details Camp.	msg
LINE to PIERREMANDE	28th	—	The Battalion was relieved by the troops of 12th London Regt (1st & 2 Coys) and by 1 Coy of 8th Bn London Regt. Relief reported complete 11.30 p.m. Battalion marched back to PIERREMANDE. Strength of battalion on 28/2/18 58 officers 946 O.R. Wets went 44 Off. 795 O.R.	msg APPENDIX C

H.W.R. Jones
Lieut & Adjutant

APPENDIX A

SECRET.   OPERATION ORDER NO. 1.   Copy No. 14
          6TH BN LONDON REGIMENT.   7/2/18.

Ref. Map Sheet.
AMIENS 17   Reveille   4 a.m.
1/100,000   Breakfast   4.45 a.m.
ST QUENTIN 18
1/100,000

1. The Battn. will move to-morrow the 8th inst to ARBLINCOURT, DICHANCOURT and MARIZELLE.
   Order of March :-   "B" Coy.
                           "C" Coy.
                           "D" Coy.
                           H.Q. Details.
                           "A" Coy.
   The Battalion will be formed up in Column of Route on the DEMUIN VILLERS-BRETONNEUX road 200yds S. of the cross-road ¼ mile N. of LEMUIN, ready to move off at 6.5 a.m. Markers will report to R.S.M. at 5.50 a.m.

2. Dress :- Full marching order. One blanket per man will be carried.
   Steel helmets will be worn.
   Unexpended portion of day's ration for 8th inst and the dry ration for the following day will be carried.

3. Battalion Entraining and Detraining Officer - 2/Lt Kidson.

4. Route :- By march route to VILLERS-BRETONNEUX, thence by train to APPILLY, thence by march route to destination (via BRETIGNY and MANICAMP).
   Distance of 250yds between Coys. will be maintained when marching from APPILLY to new area.

5. Blankets :- One blanket per man will be tightly rolled in bundles of ten, labelled and stacked at Q.M.Stores by 5.15 a.m. Coy. Orderly Room boxes should be taken to Q.M.Stores ready for loading by 5.15 a.m.
   Officers' kits must be stacked at Q.M.Stores by 5.15 a.m. to-morrow punctually. Mess boxes must be packed by the same hour.
   Medical stores will be loaded on the maltese cart by 5.30 a.m.

6. Os.C. Coys. will render certificates re cleanliness of billets by 5.30 a.m.

7. Entraining States will be submitted to Bn. Orderly Room by 5.15 a.m. punctually.
   The Entraining Officer will collect Bn. Entraining States from the Orderly Room at 5.40 a.m. These will be handed in triplicate to Brigade Entraining Officer to Brigade Entraining Officer at VILLERS-BRETONNEUX. Marching Out states will be rendered to the Orderly Room by 5.15 a.m. Marching In States will be rendered as soon as possible after arrival in new area.

8. Lieut. Lovett will be in charge of the Transport travelling on the omnibus train and will be responsible that the wagons and lorries are guided to the correct destination from APPILLY. The three N.C.Os. and fifteen men detailed by O.C. "C" Coy. to act as unloading party will report to Lieut. Lovett at APPILLY.

9. O.C. "D" Coy. will detail one Sgt. and twenty other ranks to report to Lieut. Crofts at VILLERS-BRETONNEUX station at 9.30 a.m. to load the Omnibus Train. This party will also act as unloading party and will report to the Brigade Detraining Officer on arrival.

10. Instructions re Transport going by Omnibus Train have been issued separately.

(Over :-

SECRET   APPENDIX B   Copy No. 10
Ref Map 1/70" N.W.   8/2/18

Order No. 2

6th Bn, London Regiment

1. **RELIEF**   The Bn will relieve the 12th Bn, Manchester Regt in the central sub-sector tomorrow.
2. **STARTING POINT** Bridge G.9.a.1.7
3. **ORDER OF MARCH**   C Company
                          D
                          A
                          B
                          HQuarters

Leading company will pass the starting point at 5pm.

ROUTE Road junction G.9.c.2.2 & H.1.c.8.4 where guides will be met. 250yds between companies as far as BUTTES DE WARLY. Forward of this 50yds between platoons.

GUIDES will be met at H.1.c.8.4 and will consist 1 per

(2)

platoon, 1 per company HQ and 1 per Batln. H.Q.

"A" Coy, 6th Londons will relieve one Coy, 18th Manchesters as Right Support Coy.
"B" Coy,   do   do   do   Left   do.
"C" Coy,   do   do   do   Right Front Coy
"D" Coy,   do   do   do   Left   do

6. **DRESS**. Full marching order, one blanket rolled. Steel helmets will be worn, box respirators in alert position.

7. **BLANKETS**. One blanket per man will be tightly rolled in bundles of 10, labelled & stacked at Q.M. stores not later than 3pm. Disciplinary action will be taken if this order is not strictly complied with.

8. **TRENCH STORES** will be drawn from Q.M. stores at 10am

9. **LEWIS GUNS** and 20 drums per gun will be drawn as early as possible, cleaned & inspected under the direction of Sgt DRAGE who will report to Orderly Room on completion.

10. R.S.O. will instruct all signallers as to signalling systems to to be used.

(3)

11. All trench stores, aeroplane photographs, special maps, defence schemes & will be taken over from unit relieved and receipts forwarded to Bn HQ within 6 hours of relief.

12. Completion of relief will be notified to Bn HQ by the code word "TURCO"

13. Marching out states will be rendered to reach Bn Orderly Room by 4pm

14. Billets will be left in a clean & sanitary condition & certificates to this effect will be rendered by O.C. Coys & O/c HQ Details by 4pm

15. ACKNOWLEDGE

P. Doyle
Capt & A/Adjt
6th Bn. London Regt.

Copies to :-
1. Commanding Officer
2. Second in Command
3. OC "A" Coy
4. OC "B" Coy
5. OC "C" Coy
6. OC "D" Coy
7. O/c HQ Details
8. Q.M & T.O.
9. Medical Officer
10. 18th Bn Manchester Regt.
11. Intelligence Officer
12. War Diary
13. File

SECRET. OPERATION ORDER NO. 5. Copy No. 4
8TH BN. LONDON REGIMENT. 27/8/18

WAR DIARY
APPENDIX C

1. On night of 28th/1st the 8th Battalion London Regiment will be relieved as follows :-
    North of LAIN DU DONCHER (exclusive) by 12th Battalion London Regiment (less two Coys.).
    South of LAIN DU DONCHER (inclusive) by one Coy. 8th Battalion London Regiment.

2. (A) "D" Coy. 12th Battalion will relieve "A" Coy. 8th Battalion.
    "C" Coy. do. do. do. "C" Coy. do.

    Platoons will relieve as follows :-
    No. Platoon 12th Bn. will relieve No. Platoon 8th Bn.
    No.   "   "   "   "   "   "   "   "
    No.   "   "   "   "   "   "   "   "
    No.   "   "   "   "   "   "   "   "
    No.   "   "   "   "   "   "   "   "
    No.   "   "   "   "   "   "   "   "
    No.   "   "   "   "   "   "   "   "

   (B) One Coy. 8th Bn. will relieve "B" Coy. plus one Platoon of "D" Coy.
    Platoon reliefs will take place as follows :-
    No. 5 Platoon 8th Bn. will relieve No. 14 Platoon 8th Bn.
    No. 6   "   "   "   "   "   15   "   "   "
    half No. 7   "   "   "   "   "   16   "   "   "
    half No. 7   "   "   "   "   "   10   "   "   "
    No. 8   "   "   "   "   "   11   "   "   "

   (C) "B" Coy. will not be relieved but will remain in position until relief of forward Coys. is complete.

3. (A) O.C. "A" Coy. and O.C. "C" Coy. will detail one N.C.O. to act as guide for each platoon of 12th Bn. which is taking over any of their Coy. area, also one guide for each Coy. H.Q. These guides will wait at cross-roads at N.U.c.7.7. at 6.0 p.m. on 28th inst. for 12th Bn. and will lead platoons of 12th Bn. to Platoon H.Q. of platoons to be relieved.
    Each guide must be instructed which platoon of 12th Bn. he is to meet and by what route he is to lead it in.
    Guides for each post will be at their platoon H.Q.

   (B) O.C. "B" Coy. will detail 5 N.C.Os. to act as guides for the relieving platoons of 8th Bn. and will be responsible for guiding No. 8 Platoon of 8th Battalion to Platoon H.Q. of No. 11 Platoon "C" Coy.
    These guides will be at road junction N.14.A.II.48. at 7.15 p.m. on 28th inst. They must be instructed which platoon of 8th Battalion they are to guide and must know the best route to Platoon H.Q.
    Guides for each post will be at their platoon H.Q.

- 2 -

4. The following must be carefully handed over :-
   (a) Defence Scheme, sketch maps, and standing orders.
   (b) Work in progress, proposed work both on forward
       positions and keeps.
   (c) Trench Stores, reserves of rations and S.A.A. Receipts
       to be forwarded to Battalion Orderly Room within 12
       hours of relief.
   (d) Information regarding daylight approaches forward, and
       avoidance of movement under enemy observation.

5. Reliefs will be reported complete by wiring the alphabetical
   letter of the paragraph of these orders which concerns the
   relief in question.
            (i.e. "A" for relief by 7th Loyton Regt.
             "B" "   "   " 8th   "   ").

6. Each platoon when relieved will move off under the platoon
   commander to billets in PITMAAMAIX.

7. Route.
   Crossroads at N.9.d.80.85. - NORD de B'SPINOIR - NORD
   D'ORNEAU - PITMAAMAIE.
   The Intelligence Officer will arrange for this to be
   picqueted at the various cross-roads by men of Bn. Patrolling
   Platoon.

8. Guides.
   2/Lt. S.M.Hodges is in charge of billeting arrangements.
   The following will meet Coy. at road junction C.20.a.5.1. :-
        One C.9.M.S. per Coy. and one for H.Q.Details.
        One guide per Platoon and one for each section of M.G.
                                        billeted separately.
        One guide per Coy. and one for H.Q. to show Officers
   their billets.

9. All Lewis Guns will be taken after relief to B.H.Q. to be
   formed on the road opposite Battalion Orderly Room by No. 1
   of the L.G.Team, who will remain with his gun, and after
   loading it on the limber will march to PITMAAMAIE behind the
   limber.   The L.G.Sgt. will supervise the packing of these
   Lewis Guns.

10. Coy. and H.Q.Mess boxes must be packed and stacked on road
    outside H.Q.Mess by 8.30 p.m. 26th inst. One Sergeant per
    Coy. should proceed with limber collecting them.
    The Medical Cart will be on the road opposite Bn. H.Q. at
    8.30 p.m. 26th inst. to be loaded by Medical Officer's staff.
    Bn. Orderly Room boxes will be loaded on limber at 8.30 p.m.
    26th inst.
       All other stores, including Armourer's, Bootmakers' and
    Tailors' stores will be loaded on the ration limbers to-night.
    Horses will move Cookers and Watercarts about 6.00 p.m. 26th
    inst.

11. Coy. Commanders' servants will be at cross roads at N.9.d.80.85
    at 7.30 p.m. 26th inst.

11.   Chargers for C.O. will be at Bn. H.Q. at 2 p.m. 29th inst.

12.   Marching In States will be rendered as soon after arrival in the new area as possible.

13.   Acknowledge.

                        (sd) H. JONES

                        Lieutenant and A/Adjutant,
                        6th Bn. London Regiment

Copies to :-
    1. Commanding Officer.
    2. Second in Command.
    3. O.C. "A" Coy.
    4. O.C. "B" Coy.
    5. O.C. "C" Coy.
    6. O.C. "D" Coy.
    7. O. i/c H.Q. Details.
    8. Transport Officer.
    9. Quartermaster.
    10. 2/Lt. Howell.
    11. O.C. 8th Bn. London Regt.
    12. O.C. 18th Bn. London Regt.
    13. File.
    14. War Diary.
    15. "   "

Army Form C. 2118.

WAR DIARY
or
INTELLIGENCE SUMMARY.
(Erase heading not required.)

6th London Regt

Vol 15

Instructions regarding War Diaries and Intelligence Summaries are contained in F. S. Regs., Part II. and the Staff Manual respectively. Title pages will be prepared in manuscript.

Place	Date	Hour	Summary of Events and Information	Remarks and references to Appendices
PIERREMANDE	1st March 1918		Battn relieved 7th Bn London Regt in the Battle Zone. A, C and D Coys moved to Battle Zone, B Coy remained at PIERREMANDE in Brigade Reserve. Battn HQ remained at PIERREMANDE.	App I
PIERREMANDE and BATTLE ZONE	1st to 20c		Battalion remained in the Battle Zone and did working parties - A, C and D Coys in their coy locality, B Coy wiring Hill 98, 1000 yards NW of BARISIS.	Nil
"	8c		2" Lieut BRENTFORD C.G. and 3 O.R. wounded.	Nil
"	12c		1 O.R. wounded (died of wounds)	Nil
"	18c		Bn Hdqrs moved from PIERREMANDE to BATTLE ZONE.	Nil
"	20st		Enemy attacked on left of 58th Divisional Front. Barrage opened 4.30 am. B Coy ordered to move to Battle positions at 5.35 am. Details remained at PIERREMANDE. 1 O.R. killed	Nil
St PAUL AU BOIS	26c		Battalion moved from BATTLE ZONE to St PAUL AU BOIS by march route. Accommodated in billets.	App 2
"	27-29c		Work on new line West of OISE and AISNE CANAL. Lieut Col C.B. Benson D.S.O. placed in charge of all troops of 174" Inf Bde West of the Canal.	Nil
"	28c		2 O.R. killed. 7 wounded (1 died of wounds)	Nil
"	29c		Band C Coys moved to Forward Zone relieving two coys of 7th Bn London Regt in BARISIS Sector.	App 3
"	30c		A, D Coys and Bn Hdqrs moved to Forward Zone, BARISIS Sector relieving remainder of	

T2134. Wt. W708—776. 500000. 4/16. Sir J. C. & B.

WAR DIARY
or
INTELLIGENCE SUMMARY.
(Erase heading not required.)

Army Form C. 2118.

Date	Hour	Summary of Events and Information	Remarks and references to Appendices
30		7" Battn London Regt. Relief complete 1.35 am.	
		Lieut. Col. C.B. Benson remained at S: PAUL to hand over work on line (West of	
		OISE – AISNE CANAL. Major W.J. Whitehead D.S.O. assumed command of the Battalion.	
		Transport lines and J.M. stores moved to S: AUBIN.	

174th Inf.Bde.
58th Div.

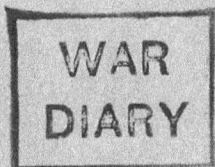

6th BATTN. THE LONDON REGIMENT.

A P R I L

1 9 1 8

Attached:

Appendices A, A.1, B,
C, D, E & F.

WAR DIARY
of
INTELLIGENCE SUMMARY.

Army Form C. 2118.

6th London Regt.   Vol. 16

Place	Date	Hour	Summary of Events and Information	Remarks and references to Appendices
	April 1918			
Man Bonavis	1/2		Relieved by 21st Irish Regt in line and marched to PIERREMANDE. Lt. Col. C.B.BENSON D.S.O. re-assumed command of Battalion.	App. A
VILLERS BRETONNEUX	2/3		Moved by march route and bus to VIC SUR AISNE and by train to LONGUEAU. Casualties 2 O.R. wounded at duty.	App. A.1.
	3		Marched to VILLERS BRETONNEUX and accommodated in billets. Transport Lines at GLISY.	
	4		VILLERS BRETONNEUX heavily shelled from 11.30 a.m. Two companies to line with HQ at VILLERS BRETONNEUX. Narrative of events to attached.	App. B and C.
			Casualties:- 2/Lt. J.GUTHRIE KILLED. DIED OF WOUNDS - 2/Lt. M.W.SARGENT. WOUNDED: MAJOR W.J. WHITEHEAD D.S.O., Capt. E.MARTIN, Capt. C.B.MAXTED M.C., Capt. E.G.GODFREY M.C. Capt. F.HILL D.C.M., Lieut. D.W.VICK, Lieut. S.W.H. PICKWORTH, 2/Lt. F.G.EPPS. 2/Lt. J.R.CAWTE, 2/Lt. H.J.PLUNKETT M.C., 2/Lt. A.E.SCOTT M.C. (missing) 2 O.Ranks. Killed 14. Wounded 88. Wounded at duty 2. Missing 2.	
	5		H.Q. to new position S.E. of VILLERS BRETONNEUX	
BOVES	6		Two companies still to BOVES accommodated in billets. In reserve to 18th Division. Lt. C. FLADGATE wounded. 1 O.R. wounded.	
	7		Two companies to BOVES accommodated in billets. In reserve to 18th Division.	

Army Form C. 2118.

Page 2

WAR DIARY
INTELLIGENCE SUMMARY
(Erase heading not required.)

Instructions regarding War Diaries and Intelligence Summaries are contained in F.S. Regs., Part II. and the Staff Manual respectively. Title pages will be prepared in manuscript.

Place	Date	Hour	Summary of Events and Information	Remarks and references to Appendices
	April 1918			
BOVES	7		Transport lines from GLISY to CAGNY.	
	9.		Relieved 10th Bn. London Regt in support at O.34. central.	App. D.
	10.		1 O.R. wounded.	
	11.		Capt. R.J. LATHBURY wounded at duty.	
			Battle surplus of 5 Officers and 70 O.R. to 3rd Corps R.T. Camp. LONGPRÉS	
			5 O.R wounded.	
VILLERS BRETONNEUX	13		Relieved 12th Bn. London Regt in front line at VILLERS BRETONNEUX	App. E
			2 O.R. wounded (gassed)	
			Draft of 62 O.R. reported for duty.	
	15		Major C. JOHNSON, 8th Bn. London Regt reported for duty as Second in Command.	
	16.		Draft of 45 O.R. reported for duty.	
			Casualties. 2nt E.F.G. CARTWRIGHT wounded. 3 O.R. killed. 1 O.R wounded	
	17		Relieved by 9th Bn London Regt. To Res. Reserve in O.34 central	
			Shelled with gas shells from 5.30am and 5.30pm to 6.15pm. Then Bn moved to embankment 200 x N.	
			Casualties. Officers wounded (gassed) Capt & Adjt R. WYLIE Capt. R.J LATHBURY.	

WAR DIARY or INTELLIGENCE SUMMARY

Army Form C. 2118.

page 3

(Erase heading not required.)

Place	Date	Hour	Summary of Events and Information	Remarks and references to Appendices
	April 1918			
	17		Lieut & Adjt. H.M.R. JONES 2/Lt A.C. JOHNSTON 2/Lt J.S.R. LOVE 2/Lt L.F. WHEELER	
			2/Lt J.E. ROSE 2/Lt W.E. BINGER 2/Lt R.H. RIANT 2/Lt H.J. WEBB	
			O/Ranks. Died of wounds 1. Wounded (gassed) 390	
BOVES		10.0 pm	Proceeded by Bus to BOVES, accommodated in billets. Remained in Bde. Reserve	
BOUTILLERIE	19		Move by march route to BOUTILLERIE	App F
			Major C. JOHNSON returned to duty with 8th Bn London Regt.	
	24		5 O/R killed and 12 O/R wounded by shell fire	
	25		Training and organization of drafts received.	
BELLANCOURT	26.		Moved to BELLANCOURT by Bus and accommodated in billets	App H
			Transport moved by march route, stayed night 26/27 at CROUY and arrived at BELLANCOURT 27/4/18.	
	29.		Twelve (Battle surplus) reported for duty.	
			Regt of 2 officer and 50 O.R. reported.	
			Lt. Col. C.B. BENSON DSO. assumed temporary command of 174th Inf. Bde.	
			Capt. B. BURT-SMITH M.C. assumed temporary command of Battalion.	
	27/30		Refitting. Reorganization and training carried on	

Army Form C. 2118.

page 4

WAR DIARY

INTELLIGENCE SUMMARY.

(Erase heading not required.)

Instructions regarding War Diaries and Intelligence Summaries are contained in F. S. Regs., Part II. and the Staff Manual respectively. Title pages will be prepared in manuscript.

Place	Date	Hour	Summary of Events and Information	Remarks and references to Appendices
	April 1918			
BELLANCOURT	30		Strength of unit :- 27 Officers 795 O.Ranks. includes 182 posted but not joined. Number present with Battalion. 17 Officers 534 O.Ranks.	

C M Butt
2nd Lieut & Acty Adjutant
6th Bn. London Regt.

APPENDICES

A
A.1
B
C
D
E
F

SECRET.   Copy No A

Operation Order P[?]   18
by
Major W. J. Whitehead

[stamp: 1/5 BATTALION ORDERLY ROOM 20 APR 1918 A860 CITY OF LONDON RIFLES]

1. This Battalion will be relieved by 215th French Regt tonight.

2. Coy Commanders will each provide guides for incoming Battalion as detailed by Commanding Officer this Battalion. Each Company will detail one Officer, one NCO per platoon, one OR per post to remain behind for 24 hours. These, on completion of this time, or when released by the French Comdt will assemble at Bn Battle Zone HQ and form the Battalion under the charge of senior officer present.

3. Order of relief will be as detailed by Commanding Officer this morning.

4. O.C. A & D Coys will each send an Officer to report to O.C. Coy. 4th Suffolk Regt, Rond D'Orleans when their last platoon has passed Rond D'Orleans. The 4th Suffolks will move off when both Officers have reported.

5. Lewis Guns, 16 drums per gun, will be carried, the remainder loaded on limbers. Gun teams at present attached to H.Q. will carry

(2)

their guns & drums.

6. Receipts will be obtained for all trench stores as detailed, maps be handed over to incoming battalion. Receipts must also be obtained from the French for S.A.A. re left on dumps.

7. Completion of relief will be reported to this Office by the code word DARK.

8. On completion of relief, companies will proceed to Pervemande independently, where guides & billeting party will be met.

9. Companies will report immediately on arrival at destination.

10. ACKNOWLEDGE.

(Sd) R WYLIE
Capt and a/Adjt

Copies issued to:
1. Commanding Officer
2. OC 'A' Coy
3. OC 'B' Coy
4. OC 'C' Coy
5. OC 'D' Coy
6. O/C HQ Details
7. Comdt, 215th French Regt.
8. QM
9. File
10. War Diary
11. War Diary

SECRET

6th Bn London Rgt.
Operation Order P 5

A/2rA
Copy No 2
9/4/1918

Ref maps
sheet 70D 70E

1. The Battalion will move to an assembly point at X.16.c. whence it will proceed to an entraining station at VIC ST AISNE.

2. Route. PONT D'ASS'T BRIDGE M.93. BARTEL FARM. RUE DE NOYON. ST PAUL. ST. AUBIN. LATOUR FM.

3. Starting point. S. end of village.

4. Order of march. A B C D HQ
Distance 200 yds between platoons to be maintained. Leading platoon of A Coy will pass starting point at 10.30 a.m.

5. Dress. Full marching order. Unexpended portion of today's rations and rations for following day will be carried.

6. Usual halts will be observed.

7. Marching Out States (one hour before moving off). Usual entraining states and marching in states will be rendered.

8. Acknowledge.

B.

NARRATIVE OF EVENTS OF 6th.Bn.LOND. REGIMENT
FROM MIDNIGHT 2/3rd.APRIL TO 3.30 a.m. 7th.APRIL 1918.

The Battalion left VIG-EN-AIRE by train about midnight 2/3rd.April 1918, arriving at LONGUEAU at 2.30 p.m. on the 3rd. Through some misunderstanding as to destination of the train there was no one to meet the Battalion on arrival, and consequently no orders. After some time I got on to 5th.Army and 2nd. ? Corps by telephone, and was informed that the battalion under my command was attached to 18th.Division. On reference to 18th.Division I was informed that I was to proceed to VILLERS BRETONNEUX and that a Staff Officer would be sent to me by car with written orders. These orders, which have been destroyed, instructed me to march to VILLERS-BRETONNEUX for accomodation there on night of 3/4th. and for relief of 35th.Bn.A.I.F. on night of 4/5th.
On receipt of these orders, and after having the situation explained to me by Capt.Mitchell, 18th.Division, who arrived with the Staff Officer of 18th.Division, I ordered the transport to GLIZY there to find accomodation for themselves, and left Major Whitehead in charge of the battalion with orders to proceed to VILLERS BRETONNEUX by the main road, LONGUEAU - VILLERS BRETONNEUX, but not to pass the point O.26.d.5.4 until dark. I myself proceeded direct to 18th.Div.Advanced H.Q. at BUSSELLES to try and procure maps of the area, more detailed information of the situation, and my role up to the time I relieved the 35th.Bn. A.I.F. in the line. Having got all the information I could I proceeded to VILLERS BRETONNEUX at which place the battalion arrived about midnight 3/4th. and were accomodated in billets. On arrival I reported myself to Lieut.Colonel GODDARD, 35th.Bn. A.I.F. who was in command of the kws line and was acting as Advanced H.Q. to 9th.Brigade A.I.F. He explained the front line and how it was held. I established my H.Q. in a house near Cross Roads in O.35.b.8.5. During this time and until 4.30 a.m. on the 4th. the situation was quiet. At 4.30 a.m. hostile artillery commenced to shell the village but not heavily, at 8 a.m. as the artillery fire was becoming more intense I moved Battn.H.Q. to those of Lieut.Colonel Goddard so as to be more closely in touch with the situation and the battalion moved into cellars to get better protection. The location of units on the morning of 4th. inst are given on the attached Location Report marked.

NARRATIVE OF BATTLE ON 4th.

From reports received by Lieut.Colonel GODDARD it appears that the enemy attacked at 5.30 a.m., and the front line held.
At 9 a.m. I received an order from 55th.Brigade saying I was placed under their orders in case of need. Immediately one officer and two runners were despatched to their H.Q. at V..a...6 for liason. (Message marked A).
At about 10.45 a.m. I was ordered to send one company to 7th. Buffs H.Q. to come under the orders of the C.O. of that battalion I accordingly sent "B" Company who under orders of O.C.7th.Buffs took up a position facing E at W.1.b.50.05 and formed a reserve to 7th.Buffs. This company was in position at about 11.30 a.m. (Message marked B)
At about 11 a.m. Lieut.Colonel GODDARD informed me that 35th. Bn. A.I.F. were fighting on their support line and that his line was then approximately P.27.d.40.90 to V.2 Central. After that time several runners from the then front line reported that the mens rifles and Lewis guns were very clogged with mud. I accordingly sent up 8 Lewis Guns with 100 Drums and spare parts to 35th.Bn. A.I.F. to be exchanged for dirty and damaged guns of that battalion. The carrying party consisted of 2 N.C.O's and 10 men of the Battle Patrol and 8 Lewis Gunners, this party

/guided

guided by Australian runners left Battn. H.Q. at about 2 p.m., handed over the guns and brought back 8 dirty guns and 100 drums which they handed over to H.Q. 35th.Bn. A.I.F. at about 3.35 p.m. The losses of the carrying party were 2 killed and 5 wounded.
The casualties of the battalion at 2.15 p.m. were approximately 8 Officers wounded and 30 O.R. killed or wounded. At about 3 p.m. the line ran as follows, P.31.a.40.00 - P.25.d.30.00 - P.31.b.50.00 - V.3.7 with apparently the original line of 55th.Brigade still holding.

At 3 p.m. I was ordered to 53rd.Brigade H.Q. at the MONUMENT, V.6.a.5.5, I accordingly went there and left my Adjutant, Capt. Wylie, in charge of the battalion in my absence.
At approximately 3.30 p.m. for no apparent reason, unless the flanks further N & S were turned, the whole front line as then held commenced to withdraw, from what I can gather the withdrawal commenced from the right. Meanwhile VILLERS-BRETONNEUX and Brigade H.Q. were being very heavily shelled with H.E. and sneezing gas. "D" Company of this battalion covered the withdrawal of 7th.Buffs and finding themselves unsupported on either flank slowly withdrew to U.6.b, they were not closely pressed by the enemy, and the Captain of this company reported that there appeared to be more men withdrawing than enemy advancing.

At about 4 p.m. 53th.Brigade H.Q. received news that their line had been broken and accordingly withdrew from the house in which their H.Q. were to about U.3.c.50.00 where they formed up Brigade H.Q.Details facing E and tried to reform the men coming through them on a line running N & S through this point.

At this hour (4 p.m.) the battalion was disposed as follows :-
"D" Company in U.6.b facing E and covering the road.
Remaining companies and Battn.H.Q. in VILLERS BRETONNEUX standing by. News reached Lieut.Colonel GODDARD about the same time that his line was broken, and he ordered Capt.Wylie to defend the village and withdrew with his H.Q. to about O.34.d. The remaining companies and all Battn.H.Q. were turned out, and in from ¼ hr. to 30 minutes A Company was clear of the village. The following was the position :-
"D" Company at O.36.b
"A" " on right of "D" Company.
"C" " debouching at O.36.C.Central.
"B" " slightly E of O.36.C.Central.
About two troops of cavalry at O.36.b.
One Lewis Gun and 8 men of an Australian Battn at O.35.b.8.5.
The cooks and snipers of this battalion patrolling the village.

Meanwhile 36th.Bn A.I.F. had arrived and were in artillery formation on a line running approximately N & S through U.5.b.Central. They were there at about 4.10 p.m. and it is not known whence they arrived. The Commanding Officer of this battalion decided to counter-attack between U.6.c.5.4 and the railway in O.36.c. At this time the enemy were in Brigade H.Q. near the MONUMENT with a machine gun mounted there and also about U.3.c.5.3 with a machine gun.
An enemy patrol also about this time was reported to have approached the railway bridge in O.36.c which an R.E.Officer was attempting to destroy. This patrol was driven off by "C" Company of this battalion.

The counter-attack of 36th.Bn. A.I.F. was got under way very rapidly and efficiently, and the whole battalion were advancing by 4.30 p.m. The counter-attack passed through, assisted N of the railway by apparently other Australians troops and British Cavalry. "A" & "D" Companies of this battalion followed 36th.Bn. A.I.F. and formed a 2nd. wave. The railway being reached by shortly afterwards A.I.F. Seeing that the right flank of the Australians was exposed, Capt.Lathbury moved up "A" & "D" Companies of this battalion on the right of the Australians, facing S.E. and kept touch with the Australians on his right and left.

/Meanwhile

Meanwhile on the N of the railway the sequence of events are more difficult to follow. Apparently one or two companies of Australians counter-attacked N of the railway and in line with the 36th.Bn. A.I.F., and started shortly before B & C companies of this battalion debouched from the village. On debouching from the village B & C Companies seeing our own troops in front of them and under a very considerable machine gun barrage, advanced by rushes and took up a supporting position running from the houses in O.36.b.60.00 southwards to the railway. They got into touch with about 2 troops of cavalry at O.36.b.00.30 and Australian troops to their front.

During the counter-attack cavalry got touch with Battn.H.Q. in VILLERS BRETONNEUX and reported that they had 300 men available in case of necessity.

At 1 a.m. 5th.April one or two companies of 36th.Bn.A.I.F. and about a similar number of, it is believed the 33rd.Bn. A.I.F.made a silent advance E on a line N & S of railway bridge in U.1.b. They advanced about 200 yards and took three or four machine guns and some 12 prisoners. This advance had the effect of creating a gap between the party that advanced and "A" & "D" Companies of this battalion. Capt.Lathbury, the Senior Officer of A & D Companies, accordingly extended further and filled the gap.
This completed the counter-attack and established one forward line as follows:- U.6.c.5.4 - V.1.Central - V.1.b.9.5 x P.26.c.00.25.

The greatest credit is due to O.C.36th.Bn.A.I.F. bwho organized and launched the counter-attack, and to his battalion for the spirited way in which it was carried out. This officer undoubtedly retrieved a very awkward situation.

At 2 a.m. on 5th. I withdrew B Company from O.36.b.60.00 and brought them to the Sunken Road in U.5.a.7.5 to act as a Reserve Company to the line S of the railway. At the same time I sent one platoon of "A" Company, who had become detached from its company during the attack, plus the Sapping Platoon to U.6.c.5.4 to extend and strengthen the right flank. These moves were decided on in consultation with O.C. 36th.Bn. A.I.F. Battn.H.Q.also were established with those of 36th.Bn.A.I.F. on road in U.5.a.70.25.

The disposition of the battalion at 4 a.m. on 5th.April was therefore as follows:-
Battn.H.Q. at U.5.a.70.25
Sapping Platoon and one platoon "A"Coy at U.6.c.5.4.
A & D Companies facing S.E. & E in V.1.a.& b.
C Company at O.36.b.00.60
B " in Reserve at U.5.a.7.5.

During the early morning of 5th.the enemy were seen to be massing at various points of the front but were dispersed by Lewis Gun fire, with considerable loss it is believed.

The battalion was to have been re-organized on night of 5th. but relief orders arrived which resulted in H.Q., B Coy, C Coy, Sapping Platoon and one platoon of A Company being relieved on the early morning of the 6th, and the remaining companies, A & D, on the early morning of 7th.

The total casualties of the battalion for the period covered were:-

        Officers.   14 wounded.
        Other Ranks. 13 Killed.
                        97 Wounded.
                         9 Missing.
    Total. 14 Officers 119 O.R.

GENERAL REMARKS.

1. Throughout the enemy were very active with snipers and machine guns and no one could approach our front line posts by day. Our snipers must be very active to keep the enemy snipers down. The enemy use trees a good deal for sniping purposes.

2. There is, or was, no proper trench line on our present front, and no wire in front of our positions.

3. Good artillery targets were frequently offered, but there was no means of getting on to the artillery rapidly from Battn.H.Q.

4. E.A. were conspicuous for their absence, ours were continually over us flying low.

5. The feeding of troops in the front line presents difficulties and Tommy Cookers are required.

6. A service of mounted orderlies is required for rapid transmission of messages.

7. Arrangements for the evacuation of wounded were inadequate. A report by my M.O. on the subject is attached marked "C".

8. During the attack the enemy showed white Very Lights to signify a gain of ground or a tactical feature. It is suggested that our troops should use the same lights to deceive the enemy as to his position.

9. Enemy machine guns were very efficient and got quickly into action, it is suggested that reserves close at hand are necessary to rapidly round these up and restore lost ground. The enemy used M.G. barrage considerably and covered reverse slopes with such fire.

10. It is suggested that the counter-attack battalion should be as far forward as possible and clear of villages and main lines of approach.

11. Hostile artillery was concentrated on villages, exits and main line of approaches. O.28.d. - O.34.c - the railway at V.1.a and VILLERS BRETONNEUX received special attention. Any battalion moving up from BOIS L'ABBE could not debouch without serious losses between O.28 Central and O.34.Central.
During the attack except on selected localities hostile artillery fire was not heavy. Hostile artillery lifted directly the enemy fired a white very light.

12. VILLERS BRETONNEUX is not a suitable place for Battn. H.Q. on account of the shelling and the consequent difficulty of communication.

13. Precautions against mud clogging Lewis Guns and rifles are stil very necessary.

14. From prisoners taken the enemy's infantry appears to be a very mixed bag and are not to be compared with their artillery and machine gunners. There would appear to be no reason why the enemy cannot be held indefinitely provided,
    (a) The line is sufficiently strongly held.
    (b) Troops are not kept too long on the line and are given a chance to recuperate when out of it.
    (c) Mobile Reserves are at hand.

15. I suggest that a series of lines inadequately held, such as Forward Zone, Battle Zone, Corps Zone, Any Zone etc, only encourages troops to think that they will be left "in the air" and that the line behind them is the one that is selected to fight the enemy on. Although it is obvious that depth held by sufficient troops is correct, thin attenuated lines in breadth and depth cannot stop a determined attack and the soldier knows it. Thus the human element comes into play and and troops partially disciplined and trained cannot and will not accept the sacrifices of the old trained soldier.

From the men of 18th.Divn. I saw retiring they appeared to me to be "fed up" - they showed no fear but just walked back. It appeared to me that they had been too long in the line.

C B Buish
Lieut.Colonel.
Comdg. 6th.Bn.London Regiment.

9/4/18.

COPY.

France.
6th April 1918.

My dear Colonel,

I would like you to let this take to you my grateful appreciation and thanks for the valuable assistance rendered by yourself and battalion during enemy attack on 4th instant. The Australian troops under my command in the defence of VILLERS-BRETONNEUX were filled with admiration for your gallant 6th Londons when they responded so willingly and eagerly at a moment when the position was critical. It has given me much pleasure to embody in my report to my Brigade Commander a record of the valuable service rendered by yourself and your command.

With every good wish to your success.

I remain my dear Colonel,
Sincerely Yours,
F.W. GODDARD. Lieut.Colonel.

Lieut.Colonel.C.B.BENSON. D.S.O.
Comdg. 6th.Bn.London Regiment.

B.E.F.
16/4/18.

Dear Colonel Goddard,

I have just received your letter and I cannot express how much I and the battalion under my command appreciate the kind message you have sent us, this to us is all the more valued as we were fighting on the 4th inst with the highest class fighting troops of our Empire, namely with Australian Battalions.

I, in the name of my battalion not only thank you for the note and its kind wishes but hope that it will be our privilege to fight again with you and yours - we could not be in better company.

With all best wishes.

Yours Very Sincerely,
C.B.BENSON. Lieut.Colonel
Comdg.6th.Bn.London Regiment.

To. Lieut.Colonel.F.W.GODDARD. D.S.O.
Comdg. 35th.Battn. A.I.F.

Copy No. 8
9/4/18.

6th BN. THE LONDON REGIMENT.

ORDER NO. P.7.

1. Bn. will relieve the 10th Bn. The London Regt. in support position, O.34 central this evening. Bn. Headquarters will be O.34 central.

2. Starting Point - C. Coy. billet.

3. The Bn. will move up by half Coys. at 200 yds distance, in the following order:-
   A. B. C. D. Coys., Headquarters.
   Leading half Coy. will pass the starting point at 5-30 p.m.

4. ROUTE. BOVES - N.28.d. - main LONGEAU - VILLERS BRETONNEUX ROAD.

5. DRESS. Battle Order.

6. S.A.A. 170 rounds S.A.A. per man to be carried. Lewis Guns, magazines and trench stores will be carried.

7. Cookers, watercarts and petrol tins, rations for consumption tomorrow, etc. will be sent up tonight.

8. Cookers will prepare a hot meal which will be served at N.29.c.
   Cookers will then proceed to Transport Lines. Dixies will be taken up from this point to the support line by a limber which will be detailed by the Transport Officer to accompany the Bn.

9. Battle Surplus already detailed will return to Details Camp when the Bn. moves off.

10. 2/Lieuts. L. Allden, H.M. Hodges, C.H. Showell, N.S. Fox and Lieut. G. Harris will return to Details.
    2/Lieut. C.H.L. Bubb will take over duties of Regtl. Signalling Officer.

11. Officers' valises, Orderly Room Boxes, Mess Boxes, L.G. Boxes etc. will be stacked outside Bn. Orderly Room by 5 p.m. Each Officer should carry necessary messing utensils.

12. Billets will be left clean and tidy.

13. Relief will be reported complete by code word POODLE

14. ACKNOWLEDGE.

(sd) R. WYLIE,
Capt. & A/Adjt.

Copies issued to :-
1. Commanding Officer.
2/5 A.B.C.D. Coys.
6. O.i/c H.Q. Details.
7. Q.M. & T.O.
8/9 War Diary
10. File.

SECRET.   6th Bn London Regt.   Copy No.   E.
           Operation Order No. P.6.   13/4/18.

                                        A1035.

Map. 62.D.

1. The Battn will relieve 12th Bn London Regt. in the line to-night & will be relieved in its present position by 7th Bn.

2. Dress :- Battle Order.

3. Platoons will move at 200 yards interval. Coy Commanders will report to this Bn H.Q. before moving off.

4. The 7th Bn. will relieve in following order :—
   D — C — H.Q. — B — A.

5. Guides :- One per platoon under arrangements made by Int. Officer will be at O.27.a.2.4. at 7.55 p.m.

6. 1 N.C.O. or O.R. will meet relieving Coys of 7th Bn. & show them the billets.

7. Band & Fighting Patrol will move under command of O.C. C Coy.

8. Company Cooks will report to O/C H.Q. Details before moving off & proceed to VILLERS-BRETONNEUX with H.Q. Details.

9. Intelligence Officer will arrange for 2 snipers to be attached to each of the forward companies.

10. Each man will take two days rations, full water bottle. Each Coy. with the exception of A. Coy. will draw 33 shovels. Reserve

10) Patrol tins will be drawn as under:—
A. Coy 5. B. Coy 9. C. Coy 10. D. Coy 5.

11. Guides of 12th Bn. for Coy H.Q. each platoon, & Bn. H.Q. will meet companies at Railway Bridge O.35.a.7.1. as under:—
D. Coy   — 9 p.m.
C. "   — 9-15 p.m.
H.Q.   — 9-20 p.m.
B. Coy   — 9-30 p.m.
A. "   — 9-45 p.m.

12. O.C. B. Coy will arrange to hand over 2 Very Pistols to O.C. A. Coy & one to O.C. D. Coy. O.C. C. Coy will hand one Very Pistol to O.C. D. Coy.

13. All trench stores, S.A.A, maps etc. to be taken over from 12th Bn. & receipts in duplicate forwarded to Bn. Ord. Room as soon as possible after relief.

14. All Bivvy sheets not taken up to firing line are to be handed over to relieving companies of 7th Bn. & receipts obtained.

15. O.sC. Coys. will submit disposition maps to Bn. Orderly Room as soon as possible after relief.

16. Completion of relief to be reported as soon as possible by name of officer commanding company & time of relief.

17. This order will not be taken up into front line but must be memorised & destroyed.

18. Acknowledge.

R. Wylie.
Capt. & Adjutant

Distribution — see over.

SECRET.

6th.Bn.London Regiment.
OPERATION ORDER No.18.

Refce.Map.
Sheet 62.D.
AMIENS. 17.

1. The battalion will move by march route to MONTIERES, West of AMIENS, thence by bus.

2. Route and starting point will be notified later. The Intelligence Officer will reconnoitre the route beforehand with party of guides to show the battalion the way especially through AMIENS.

3. Order of March and enbussing :-
    H.Q. & D Coy.
    A Company.
    B "
    C "
    Intervals of 250 yards to be maintained between companies.

4. Leading company will be ready to move off at 1.30 p.m.

5. Dress :- Full Marching Order. Unexpended portion of day's rations to be carried.

6. Usual halts will be observed.

7. Blankets will be collected, tied tightly in bundles of ten and placed in Q.M.Stores for return to D.A.D.O.S. as ordered.

8. Dinners will be at 11.30am and tea on arrival in new area.

9. Each O.C.Coy will arrange to have ready on arrival at new area, billeting parties.

10. Rations for consumption 27th.inst. will be distributed at enbussing point and necessary arrangements must be made to have same rapidly distributed.

11. Officers valises to be packed ready in billets by 10.am.

12. Lewis Guns and drums, Signalling Panniers and all stores to be stacked at 10.0 am. and loaded on limbers by Coy Lewis Gunners.

13. Transport arrangements and officers chargers will be notified later.

14. Lt.C.Harris for the Battn. and Lt.T.W.Wardhaugh for Bde H.Q. will act as advance parties and on arrival in new area will report to Major.Mitchell D.A.A.G. 58th.Division, care of Town Major, SAINT NICQUIER.

15. Acknowledge.

26/4/18.
(Sd) C.H.L.BURD.
2/Lieut.A/Adjutant.

Copies issued to :-
No.1 Commanding Officer.
No.2.O.C. "A" Coy.
No.3.O.C. "B" "
No.4.O.C. "C" "
No.5.O.C. "D" "
No.6.O i/c H.Q.Details.
No.7.O.C. T.C.
No.8 File.

WAR DIARY
or
INTELLIGENCE-SUMMARY.

(Erase heading not required.)

Army Form C. 2118.

Place	Date	Hour	Summary of Events and Information	Remarks and references to Appendices
	May 1918.			
BELLANCOURT	1		Training	
	2		Draft of 161 OR joined for duty	
	5		Battle Surplus 1 Officer + 50 OR proceeded to III Corps R.T. Camp	
			Transport moved by march route to BOURDON	
MIRVAUX	6		Major N.D. LUPTON joined for duty and assumed temporary command of Battalion	
			Transport moved by march route to MIRVAUX	
			Battalion moved by march route and bus to MIRVAUX and accommodated in billets	App A
	7		Lieut Col. C.B. BENSON DSO re-assumed command of Battalion	
			Major N.D. LUPTON assumed duties of Second in Command	
	10		Lieut Col. C.B. BENSON DSO assumed temporary command of 174th Infantry Brigade	
			Seven officers joined for duty :- 2nd Lieuts. W.E. WHITE A.J. FROST H.E. HOPKINS	
			L.C. LEAPMAN S.G. HEWITT G.H. STEPHENSON W.J. MATTHEWS	
WARLOY	11		Bn. less Transport to entrainment S.W. of WARLOY into III Corps Reserve and accommodated under canvas	App A.
			Capt. E.C. GREEN reported for duty	
	11/15		Training and working parties	

Army Form C. 2118.

WAR DIARY
INTELLIGENCE SUMMARY.
(Erase heading not required.)

Page 2

Place	Date	Hour	Summary of Events and Information	Remarks and references to Appendices
	May 1918			
WARLOY	15		Battalion moved up, relieved 15 Bn. Lond Regt and took over sector of line due West from ALBERT	App. A. 2.
			Bn. HQ situated at MILLENCOURT	
	15/20		Transport lines moved to WARLOY	
			Working supplied under supervision of R.E. for general improvement of line	
	19		2nd Lt W.J. MATTHEWS killed in action	
	20		One O.Rank wounded	
			Bn HQ moved from MILLENCOURT to new position 600 yds N.	
	23		Relieved by 7th Bn London Regt. HQ and 2 Coys to HENENCOURT and 2 Coys to MELBOURNE TRENCH one mile E. of HENENCOURT. - Battn in support of Sector	App. B.
	24		One O.Rank wounded	
	26		Three O.Ranks wounded	
	27		Draft of 6 [?] O.Ranks joined for duty	
			Relieved by 10th Bn London Regt and moved to Div Reserve Huts by 9th Bn London Regt	App. C
	29		Capt. Rev. C.E. WHITEFOORD. (C.F.) wounded.	
			One O.Rank wounded	
			One O.Rank wounded at duty.	

Army Form C. 2118.

WAR DIARY
~~INTELLIGENCE SUMMARY.~~
(Erase heading not required.)

Page 3

Place	Date	Hour	Summary of Events and Information	Remarks and references to Appendices
	May 1918			
	31		Relieved by 11th Bn. R.F. in Div. Reserve and relieved 4th Bn. Devons in Corps Reserve and situated at WARLOY	App D
			Strength of Bn. 45 Officers 900 O.Ranks.	
			Numbers present 26 Officers 677 O.Ranks	
			C.H. Bell	
			2nd Lieut	
			Acting - Adjutant.	

SECRET

App. A

Copy No. 11
5/5/18.
a 1700

OPERATION ORDER No.12.

1. The Battalion will move to MOLLIENS AU BOIS by bus tomorrow.

2. EMBUSSING POINT. Junction of ABBEVILLE - ST. RICQUIER Road and NEUF MOULIN ROAD.

3. Reveille 6 a.m.   Breakfast 6-30 a.m.

4. 7-30 a.m. Bn. parade in column of route, head of column facing the well.

5. ORDER OF MARCH. Headquarters, A. B. C. D. Coys.

6. ROUTE. Cross Roads S. of S in VUACHELLES - road W. of BOIS DE L'ABBÉ.

7. Companies will maintain a distance of 200 yards. Company Commanders will ensure that the orders re numbers of busses are complied with.

8. DRESS. Full marching order - waterbottles to be filled. Steel helmets will be carried.

9. Certificates will be rendered at 6-45 a.m. that billets have been left clean and tidy.

10. ACKNOWLEDGE.

CH.L. BUBB
2/Lieut. A/ ADJT.

Distribution - Normal.

app. A.1

SECRET.
ORDER NO. 14 Copy........
10/5/18.
Ref. Map 6th BN. THE LONDON REGT.
Sheet 62D.NW. -------------------------
57 D. SW.

    Reveille   6-30 a.m.
    Sick Parade 7 a.m.
    Breakfast   7-30 a.m.

1. The Battalion will move to Corps Reserve position at C.4.b.8.3. by march route. 11/5/18.
2. <u>STARTING POINT.</u> Cross roads at T.20.d.8.2.
3. <u>ROUTE.</u> MIRVAUX - T.15.c.8.1. - T.23.c.7.1. - U.19.d.0.9. - U.20.d.2.4. - U.27.a.4.5. - C.4.b.8.3.
4. <u>ORDER OF MARCH.</u> D. Coy.
         C. Coy.
         B. Coy.
         A. Coy.
         Headquarters
  D. Coy. will pass the Starting Point at 10.30 a.m.
  Distances of 50 yds. between Platoons and 200 yds. between Coys. will be maintained. Usual halts will be observed.
5. <u>MARCHING OUT STATES.</u> will be rendered to Bn. Orderly Room by 9.45am
6. <u>BILLETS</u> will be left clean and tidy. Certficates to this effect will be handed to Bn. Orderly Room at 9-45 a.m.
  The Quartermaster will obtain from the Town Major a certificate that the billets vacated by the Bn. are in a clean condition and hand same to Orderly Room.
6. <u>OFFICERS KITS.</u> Mess Boxes, Signalling Stores and Medical Stores will be loaded on limbers at Quartermaster's Stores by 8-45 a.m.
7. <u>LEWIS GUN</u> limbers will be packed by 8 a.m. under supervision of Cpl. Macdonald.
8. <u>TRANSPORT</u> will move off at 9-30 a.m.
  N.C.Os and men earmarked for the line (as per A1341/d) will not proceed with the Battalion but will be ready to move off at short notice.

             C.H.L. BUBB,
              2/Lieut.
            Acting Adjutant,
          6th Bn. London Regiment.

Copies issued to:-
1. Commanding Officer.
2. O.C. A. Coy.
3. O.C. B. Coy.
4. O.C. C. Coy.
5. O.C. D. Coy.
6. O.i/c H.Q. Details.
7. Transport Officer
 & Quartermaster.
8. File.

SECRET   6th LONDON REGT.
                    OPERATION ORDER
                          No 15
Ref:
Sheet 57D SE
      62D NE

The 6th Bn London Regt. will be relieved by the 13th Bn London Regt.
on the night 31st/1st tonight.

1. ORDER OF RELIEF   6th Coy. will relieve   A. Coy 13th Bn
                         D   D
                         A   C
                         B   B
                         HQ

Leading platoon will leave camp at 8pm. Batt. will pass
starting point ROAD BEND V.25.d.7.6. at 8.45pm. 50yds interval
will be maintained between platoons.

2. GUIDES   The following guides will meet guides of the 13th Bn at
HENENCOURT CHATEAU at 9.30pm. 1 Guide per platoon
                                    1   "   " Coy HQ
                                    1   "   " Bn HQ

3. STORES   L. Guns will proceed in front of leading platoon of
each Coy as follows:-
                8 Lewis Guns
                32 Magazines per Gun
                Mess Boxes

All ... Signal equipment ... will be carried
back to the ... at the reserve line and the
report back to Battn HQrs. 1 L.G. teams per Coy will

4. RATIONS
    Rations for tomorrow will be issued this evening and
carried by the men to the line.
    Whilst in the line rations will leave WARLOY as soon
as ... These will be dumped in ... reserve trench
on ALBERT Road.
    Water will be sent in tins. BN Cooks will be
each ... every night at Battn HQrs.

1 Hot Meal per 24 hours will be brought up by
cookers each night.
   Tommy Cookers have been applied for.

... containers will be utilised for carrying hot tea to Coys. Rations will be carried by Ressumed Coy to front line on their way to work.

Support Coy will get their own rations.

5. **R.E. MATERIAL** Indents for R.E. Material will reach Battn HQ by 7.30am daily stating description and quantities of material required and exact locations where needed.

6. **TOOLS** All available (regimental) shovels and picks will be distributed evenly amongst companies took a view up the line.

7. **TRENCH STORES** List of trench stores taken over and countersigned will be forwarded to Battn HQ gro as soon as possible after relief.

8. **STRETCHER BEARERS** Stretcher Bearers as under will report to R.A.P. before moving off and proceed with HQ Coy
    A 2   C 1
    B 2   D 1

9. **DRESS** Battle Order will be worn. Greatcoats and haversacks will be dumped by companies in QUARRY where they will be guarded by R.M.P.
    These together with Lewis valises will be in stated place by 6.30pm.

10. **COMPLETION OF RELIEF** This will be notified to Battn HQ by wire using code word JUNE followed by time of relief.

11. **ACKNOWLEDGE**

C.H.L. BUBB Lt. Col.

1. Commanding Officer
2. OC A Coy
3. " B "
4. " C "
5. " D "
6. O/C HQ DETAILS
7. Tpt O 2nd
8. OC 18th Bn LON REGT
9. War Diary
10.
11. File

6th BN. LONDON REGT.

OPERATION ORDER

No 15

REF
Sheet 57dSE
" 62dNE

The 6th Bn London Regt will relieve the 15th Bn London Regt in the right sub-section tonight.

1. **ORDER OF RELIEF** C Coy will relieve A Coy 15th Bn
        D "   D
        A "   C
        B "   B
        HQ

Leading platoon will leave camp at 8pm. Battn will pass starting point ROAD BEND V 25 a.9.1 at 8.45pm. 50yds interval will be maintained between platoons.

2. **GUIDES** The following guides will meet platoons of the 6th Bn at HENENCOURT CHATEAU at 9.40pm. 1 Guide per platoon
            1 " Coy HQ
            1 " per HQ Coy

3. **STORES** Limbers will proceed in front of leading platoon of each Coy containing:
    1 Lewis Gun
    32 Magazines per Gun
    Mess Boxes

These stores will be dumped by Coys in the reserve line and the Limbers to return empty. 1 L.G. team per Coy will report back to Battn HQrs.

4. **RATIONS**

Rations for tomorrow will be issued this evening and carried by the men to the line.

Whilst in the line rations will leave WARLOY as soon as ready. These will be dumped on outgoing limbers near ALBERT road.

Water will be sent in tins. P.O. cans will be filled every night at Battn HQrs.

1 Hot Meal per 24 hours will be brought up by cookers each night

Tommy cookers have been applied for.

MARCH TABLE to accompany 174th Inf. Brigade Order No.18.

Serial Letter.	Date.	Unit.	From.	To.	Route.	Starting Point.	Time of passing Starting Point.	Remarks.
B.	May 15th	8th Lon.Regt. 5th Lon.Regt.	Camp in B.28.a. do.	LINE- Support ECOUST etc.	As ordered by C.O. do.	- -	- -	O.C.5th London Regt and O.C. 8th London Regt. will mutually arrange their times of march and route so that no block occurs.
C.	May 15th	174th L.T.M.B.	Camp G.11.d.	Camp B.21.c. central (2 guns to line)	Overland track G.11.d.9.9.- BEHAGNIES - MORY.	Junction of Overland Track and Track to Camps at G.12.b.3080.	12.50 p.m.	Lorries and transport of all units move as detailed in Administrative Instructions. Units will on arrival at or near halting place, at once clear the track for unit marching in rear.
		6th Lon.Regt.	Camp G.12.c.	Halting place B.28.a.	do.	do.	1.5 p.m. /·05	
		7th Lon.Regt.	Camp G.11.d.	do.	do.	do.	1.25 p.m. /·15	
		198th M.G.Coy.	Camp G.12.c.	do.	do.	do.	1.45 p.m. ?/m	
		H.Q.174th Inf.Bde.	Camp G.11.d.	L'HOMME- MORT	do.	do.	2 p.m.	Bde. H.Q. Transport will halt clear of present camp and continue march so as to reach L'HOMME MORT not before 5 p.m.
		6th Lon.Regt.	Halting place B.28.a.	Camp vacated by 8th London Regt at B.28.a.	Any	-	-	
		7th Lon.Regt.	do.	Camp vacated by 5th London Regt B.28.a.	do.	-	-	
		198th M.G.Coy.	do.	Camp for M.G.Coy. in B.28.a.	-	-	-	

(1086) Wt.W16552/M1615 250,000 Pads. 21/3/17. J.R.&C. E 685 Forms/C2122/6. App VI

Army Form C2122
(In pads of 150)

"B" Form.

MESSAGES AND SIGNALS.

No. of Message.........

Prefix.........Code.........m.	Words	Received	Sent	Office Stamp
Office of Origin and Service Instructions.		At.........m. From............. By.............	At.........m. To............. By.............	

TO	A Coy			
	D. Coy			

Sender's Number.	Day of Month.	In reply to Number.	AAA
M 252	22	-	

1. "A" Coy. will carry out an inter-company relief with "D" company today.
2. Respective company commanders will reconnoitre new positions this afternoon and will arrange all details of relief.
3. Relief will be carried out before STAND-TO in order that working parties for tonight will not be interfered with.
4. All trench stores will be properly handed over
5. Completion of relief will be notified by each company commander to this Office by the code word "LOVETT".
6. ACKNOWLEDGE

From HQZU.   R. WYLIE
Place   Capt & Adjt
Time

* This line should be erased if not required.

NOTE.

It is of the utmost importance that the first relief relief be completed as quickly as possible as the margin of time allowed for the front line Battn. to get out is very small.

Army Form C. 2118.

6 London 27

WAR DIARY

INTELLIGENCE SUMMARY.

(Erase heading not required.)

Page 1.

Place	Date	Hour	Summary of Events and Information	Remarks and references to Appendices
	June 1918.			
WARLOY	1-4		Corps Reserve holding defensive position (BAZIEUX system)	R6
	4		Lieut J.H.W. IDRIS reported for duty	R15
DAILY MAIL WOODS, CONTAY	5		Arrived at DAILY MAIL WOODS near CONTAY and accommodated under canvas	App. I & 15
	6		Training	R15
	9		2nd Lieut G.K. STEPHENSON to hospital	R15
	-		Marched past Corps Commander, in column of route	R15
	-		Transferred to G.J & Q Reserve.	R15
FOUDRINROY	10		Moved by march route and bivo to FOUDRINROY and accommodated in billets	App II & 15
	11		Training - Battalion in attack scheme, musketry, etc.	R16
	12		Inspected whilst at training by Corps Commander.	R15
	13		Lieut Colonel C.B. BENSON DSO invalided from Rear and assumed temporary command of 174th Infantry Brigade.	R15
			Captain and Adjutant R WYLIE M.C. rejoined unit and assumed duties of appointment.	R15
	14		Lieut Colonel C.B. BENSON DSO re-assumed command of battalion.	R15
			2nd Lieut A.W.N. FROST sick to hospital.	R13
	15		Training	R15

Army Form C. 2118.

WAR DIARY
or
INTELLIGENCE SUMMARY.
(Erase heading not required.)

Page 2

Place	Date	Hour	Summary of Events and Information	Remarks and references to Appendices
	June 1918			
FOURDRINOY	16		Transport moved by march route to MOLLIENS AU BOIS	Rus
LAVIEVILLE	17		Moved by bus and march route to FRANVILLERS - CONTAY Road.	} app. III Rus IV
			Relieved 1/18R Bn London Regt in Divl Reserve in LAVIEVILLE SECTOR.	
			Battle surplus sent to MIRVAUX	
LAVIEVILLE, EAST OF.	18		Relieved 15R Bn London Regt in line, right battalion, right subsector of Divl front	app V Rus
	20		2 OR killed	Rus
	21		4 OR killed. 12 OR wounded. 1 Wounded at duty	Rus
	22		Support company relieved centre front company	app VI Rus
LAVIEVILLE DEFENCE LINE	24/25		Relieved in line by 9R Bn London Regt and took over defensive position positions in LAVIEVILLE SECTOR in Divl Reserve.	app VII Rus
	26		Inter-company relief and alteration in disposition of Companies. Two companies from LAVIEVILLE LINE to BAZIEUX system and 2 companies of 9R Bn London Regt from BAZIEUX system to LAVIEVILLE LINE	Rus
			BAZIEUX system to LAVIEVILLE LINE	app VIII Rus
	28		B Company in LAVIEVILLE LINE relieved by D Company from BAZIEUX system. B Coy to BAZIEUX system	app IX Rus
	29		Practice Stand To at 11.0 am when defensive positions were held for one hour	Rus

Army Form C. 2118.

WAR DIARY
INTELLIGENCE SUMMARY.
(Erase heading not required.)

Page 3.

Instructions regarding War Diaries and Intelligence Summaries are contained in F. S. Regs., Part II. and the Staff Manual respectively. Title pages will be prepared in manuscript.

Place	Date	Hour	Summary of Events and Information	Remarks and references to Appendices
	June 1918			
LAVIEVILLE DEFENCE LINE.	30		Company Commanders reconnoitred area of right Battalion, left subsector of Divl. front.	
		26.30	Supplies Working parties	
			Strength of Battalion 44 Officers 916 O.Ranks	
			Present with Battalion 24 Officers 660 O.Ranks	
			(excluding Battle surplus)	
			Rhylie	
			Captain and Adjutant.	

app I

SECRET.   6th.Bn.London Regiment.   Copy No......
              OPERATION ORDER NO.20.   5/6/18.
※※※※※※※※※※※※※※※※※※※※※※※※※※※※※※

1. The battalion will move to "DAILY MAIL" Wood today, and remain in Corps Reserve.

2. Order of March :- H.Q. A,B, C & D Coys.

3. Starting Point :- Battn.H.Q.
Leading company will pass starting point at 3.50 p.m.
100 yds distance between platoons.

4. Dress :- Full Marching Order.

5. List of all stores left behind will be rendered to Bn.H.Q. by 7.0 p.m.

6. Mess Boxes, Lewis Guns and L.G., S.A.A. Officers valises, water-tanks and petrol tins will be stacked at Coy.H.Q. by 2.0 p.m. T.O. will arrange to collect these as soon as possible and convey to new area. Baggage wagons will proceed independently, 1st.Line transport 100 yds in rear of battalion and 26 yards between each six vehicles.

7. All men inoculated yesterday will be at H.Q. in full marching order at 2.45 p.m. and will be conveyed to new area by ambulance.

8. Rations will be delivered in new area.

9. Area will be left clean and tidy.

10. Acknowledge.

Copies issued to :-   (Sd) C.H.L.BUBB 2/Lieut.& A/Adjt.

No.1 Commanding Officer.
No.2. O.C."A" Company.
No.3. O.C."B"   "
No.4. O.C."C"   "
No.5. O.C."D"   "
No.6. O i/c H.Q.Details.
No.7. Q.M.& T.O.
No.8. File.
No.9. War diary.

App. II

SECRET.   6th.Bn.London Regiment.   Copy No....
           OPERATION ORDER NO.21.   10/6/18.

1. The battalion will proceed to new area by bus route.

2. Order of March :- H.Q., A, B, C & D Companies.

3. Battalion will parade in Mass on parade ground at 8.30 a.m. 100 yards interval will be observed between companies on on march.

4. Dress :- Full Marching Order. (Steel helmets will be carried).

5. Unexpended portion of days ration will be carried.

6. Tents and shelters will be struck and dumped in valley T.29.b.5.2. Each tent is to be packed complete, shelters to be in bundles of 20. Receipts to be forwarded to this office today.

7. Tools. One tool to every 3 men in proportion of 2 shovels to 1 pick will be issued by R.S.M.

8. Battle Surplus. Battle Surplus already detailed will accompany Battn to debussing point and there join Divl.H.Q.

Distribution normal.   (Sd) C.H.L.BUBB.
                                             2/Lieut.& A/Adjt.

SECRET. 6th. Bn. London Regiment. Copy No.....

OPERATION ORDER NO.23.

Map Sheet. 16/6/18.
62. E. & 62. D.

1. The battalion will move tomorrow morning by march route and bus to relieve a battalion of the 141st. Infantry Brigade.

2. Order of March :- A, H.Q, B, C & D Coys. Intervals of 100 yards will be observed bewteen companies.

3. Starting Point :- Road junction J.20.d.2.8. Leading company will pass starting point at 4.45 a.m.

4. Route :- J.8.d.5.8 then along road to PICQUIGNY where busses will be met.

5. Debussing Point :- CONTAY - FRANVILLERS ROAD at C.16.a.4.6.

6. Dress :- Full marching order. Steel helmets will be worn. Men will carry unexpended portion of the days ration.

7. Lewis Guns and drums will be carried.

8. On debussing, the officers who reconnoitred today will act as guides for companies. "A" Company officer will conduct H.Q.

9. Lieut. J.J. Ball will act as unit embussing officer, to whom separate orders have been issued.

10. O.C. Coys and H.Q. will render by 9.0 p.m. today embussing state showing battle surplus separately.

11. Report will be rendered to Adjutant when each company is embussed.

12. Battle Surplus will march in rear of battalion under command of Capt. Green to whom orders have been issued. Battle surplus of each company and H.Q. will parade outside Bn. Orderly Room at a time to be notified to O.C. Coys and H.Q. by Capt. Green.

13. Officers kit, mess boxes and dixies etc will be stacked outside Q.M. Stores by 4.30 a.m.

14. Billets will be left xxxxxx in a thoroughly clean and sanitary condition. 2/Lieut. A.C. Sampson M.C. will inspect all billets and will report on their state to the Adjutant at 3.45 a.m. He will then receive a certificate which he will hand to Staff Captain at Embussing Point.

15. Acknowledge.

Distribution normal. (sd) R. WYLIE Capt. & Adjt.

SECRET.   6th.Bn.London Regiment.   Copy No......

OPERATION ORDER NO.24.   17/6/18.

※※※※※※※※※※※※※※※※※※※※※※※※※

1. The battalion will move to Reserve Line at 8.45 p.m. 17/6/18.

2. Starting Point fork of valley at C.9.b.6.1.

3. Order of march "A" Coy - H.Q.-"B"-"C"-"D" Companies- 100 yds distance between platoons.

4. Route N of BOIS ROBERT - S of BAIZIEUX - N of BRESLE WOOD - CEMETRY - H.Q.

5. Headquarters is situated at D.9.b.5.6.

6. Cpl.Sharpe will guide "A" Company. Guides for companies will be met at above H.Q. on arrival of companies.

7. "STAND TO" immediately companies get into position.

8. Completion of relief will be reported to Bn.H.Q. by Company Commanders name.

9. Receipts for all trench stores, iron rations (preserved meat, groceries, biscuit rations) etc will be rendered by 11.15 p.m.

10. Rations and water will reach Bn.H.Q. by about 11 p.m. and go forward by transport to Companies dump (unless other instructions are issued) on arrival of Battn. at H.Q.

11. Mess Cart and Medical Cart will accompany Bn. also limber with dixies.

12. Tea will be issued to companies at 8 p.m.

13. Road and embankment here are to be left scrupulously clean.

14. Acknowledge.

Distribution :-   (Sd) R.WYLIE Capt.& Adjt.

Recipients of O.O.23 less
174th.Inf.Bde Tunnelling Section.

SECRET.   6th.Bn.London Regiment.   Copy No.

OPERATION ORDER NO.25.   18/6/18.

1. The battalion will be relieved by 2/2nd.Bn.London Regiment this evening and will relieve 15th.Bn.London Regiment in Right-Subsector of Right Brigade this evening.

2. Each company of 6th.Bn. will be relieved by same company of 2/2nd.Bn.London Regiment.

3. Order of relief is as follows - "C" - "B" - "D" - "A" Coys and H.Qrs.

4. Dress :- Battle Order. All trench stores will be completely handed over and full receipts obtained. These will be forwarded to this office by midday, 19th.inst.

5. "A"-"C"-"D" Coys will return to Battn.H.Q. this evening one Lewis Gun per company complete with team and ammunition to report to this Battn.Orderly Room by 9.0 p.m.

6. Three dixies per company will be carried into new position and will be sent to New Bn.H.Q. before dawn. Remaining dixies will be dumped at Company dump with greatcoats and haversacks. All cooks other than one per company will return to transport lines this evening. Remaining one per company will report to New Bn.H.Q. on arrival.

7. Officers Mess boxes etc will be at Bn.Orderly Room by 10.0 p.m. They will then be brought to New Bn.H.Q. on arrival and can be drawn from there.

8. Instructions will be given to all guards left behind in this position, as to how to find Bn.H.Q. in new position on completion of their duty. From there they will be returned to their companies.

9. Completion of relief will be forwarded to this Bn.H.Q. by code word.

10. On completion of relief companies will relieve companies of 15th.Bn.London Regiment in right subsector, as detailed this morning "START".

11. Immediately each company is relieved it will proceed independantly to its new position by best available route. For this purpose one guide per company will be at this Bn.Orderly Room by 9 p.m. to meet one guide per platoon of 15th.Bn.London Regiment who will guide the company to new position. These will at once proceed to present Coy H.Q. and stand by to await completion of first relief.

12. All trench stores, reserve rations, etc will be carefully taken over and receipts forwarded to reach this office at midday 19/6/18. Separate receipt will be given in each case for S.O.S. Signal.

13. The Battn.Lewis Gun N.C.O. will be in charge of the 3 teams reporting to Bn.H.Q. this evening and will receive verbal instructions from L.G.O.

14. Companies will mount A.A.Guns as usual.

15. When taking over, companies will obtain particulars as to ration dumps, and where rations, water, etc for tomorrow will be brought tonight.

16. Completion of relief will be forwarded to New Bn.H.Q. by code word "DONE".

17. ACKNOWLEDGE.   (Sd) R.WYLIE Captain & Adjutant.
Distribution normal & O.C.15th.Bn.London Regiment.

SECRET.　　　　　　　　6th. Bn. London Regiment.　　　　　Copy No...

App VII

Map Sheet.　　　　　　　OPERATION ORDER NO.26.　　　　　24/6/18.
SENLIS.

1. The battalion will be relieved tonight by 9th. Bn. London Regiment.

    "D" Coy 9th. Bn. will relieve "C" Coy 6th. Bn.
    "B"　"　　"　　　"　　　"　　"A"　"　　"
    "C"　"　　"　　　"　　　"　　"B"　"　　"
    "A"　"　　"　　　"　　　"　　"D"　"　　"

2. Order of relief - Right, Centre, Left, reserve companies.

3. One guide per platoon and one for Bn.H.Q. will report at these H.Q. at 9.0 p.m. without fail. These guides will be men who have today reconnoitred the route.

4. Lewis Guns and all drums brought in will be carried out. Company Commanders will render a certificate by midday tomorrow that each gun has its full complement of 32 drums. All A.A. positions will be handed over to incoming unit.

5. All trench stores, other than those brought in by us, S.A.A. etc will be handed over and receipts obtained in duplicate and forwarded to this office by 10.0 a.m. tomorrow. Particular attention will be paid to the handing over of water tins.
    Representatives of incoming unit will arrive this afternoon to take over stores. They will check the number of water tins in the line and give receipts for same. After these have been given all empty tins will be at the dump by 8.0 p.m.

6. All sickles will be returned to Bn.H.Q. by 6.0 p.m.

7. Trenches will be left clean and tidy and latrines emptied.

8. All information, dispositions, etc will be carefully handed over.

9. Completion of relief will be notified by the Company Commanders name.

10. On completion, companies will move off independently, 100 yds distance between platoons to the LAVIEVILLE SECTOR taking up the same positions as occupied night of 17/18th.

11. Rations for consumption tomorrow will be at same place as them. Water Carts will report to Coy.H.Q. and will fill petrol tins for consumption tomorrow.

12. The officer per company who proceeded to take over this sector will act as guide to the company.

13. All Lewis Guns and drums will be carried.

14. Completion of taking up new positions in LAVIEVILLE SECTOR will be reported to Bn.H.Q. by code word "HERE".

15. Acknowledge.

Distribution normal.　　　　　　　　　　　(Sd) R.WYLIE Capt. & Adjt.

SECRET.　　　　　　6th Battalion, London Regiment　　　　　app VIII
　　　　　　　　　　　　　　　　　　　　　　　　　　　　　　Copy No. 1.
　　　　　　　　　　　　OPERATION ORDER 27
Map Sheet　　　　　　　　　　　　　　　　　　　　　　　　　26/6/1918..
SENLIS 1/20000

1. C Company will relieve A Company on the front of right company as early as possible tonight.

2. All trench stores will be carefully checked and handed over and receipts forwarded to this office immediately on completion.

3. A Company after relief will return to BAZIEUX system and take up position in sector approximately in D.7.d. 2/Lt Gregory will guide company to destination.

4. A and C Coy relief must be completed by 10.0 pm and if necessary parties can be sent forward in very small numbers.

5. A Company have, this afternoon, shortened their line from AMIENS-ALBERT ROAD northwards to D.16.b.47.85 D.16.b.47.85. B Company will hold line thence northward to D.11.c.0.7.
The vacant space between B and D Coys will be occupied by A Coy 7th Bn. whilst D Coy 7th Bn. will relieve D Coy 6th Bn. Lond Rgt.

6. C Company will take over A Company's dixies. C and D Coys' dixies will be piled at Company dumps and Transport Officer will bring them to the Company lines of A and D Companies respectively in BAZIEUX.
A and D Coy cookers will be brought up to BAZIEUX.
Transport Officer will find out from Transport Officer 7th Bn, where these are sited.

7. On completion of relief by D Coy 7th Bn, D Coy 6th Bn. will return to BAZIEUX system in D.7.a and c. guided by 2/Lt. Dearsley.

8. All trench stores will be carefully handed over and receipts forwarded to this office immediately on completion. D Coy will hand over all petrol tins with trench stores.

9. Two guides from D Coy and 2 guides supplied by Intelligence Officer will report at Bn. H.Q. at 9.0. pm to lead up two companies of 7th Bn.

10. Completion of C and D Coys' first relief by 7th Bn will be reported to this office by Company Commander's name.

11. Completion of second relief will be reported by code word HERE.

12. ACKNOWLEDGE.

　　　　　　　　　　　　　　　　　　　　　　　　R. WYLIE.
　　　　　　　　　　　　　　　　　　　　　　Captain and Adjutant.

Copies issued at 5.30pm to:-
　　　　1. Commanding Officer.
　　　　2. O.C. A Coy.
　　　　3. O.C. B Coy.
　　　　4. O.C. C Coy.
　　　　5. O.C. D Coy.
　　　　6. O.C. H.Q. Details.
　　　　7. Transport Officer
　　　　　　and Quartermaster.
　　8/9. War Diary.
　　10. File.

SECRET.   6th. Bn. London Regiment.   Copy No...
OPERATION ORDER NO. 28.   28/6/18.

1. "A" Company will relieve "B" Company in line this evening.

2. One officer and 4 N.C.Os per company will proceed at once to reconnoitre and take over positions. The N.C.Os will remain and the officers will return to company in order to conduct company.

3. Working parties as detailed to "A" Coy will proceed to work taking all kit etc and on return will report to company in new position.

4. All trench stores will be carefully handed over and copies of receipts forwarded to this office by midday.

5. "B" Company cooks will remain in position and cook for "A" Company and "B" Company will take over "A" Company cooks and cooker.

6. Relief to commence as soon as possible after dusk.

7. Completion of relief will be reported by Company Commanders name.

8. Acknowledge.

(Sd) R. WYLIE Capt & Adjt.

Copies issued to :-

No. 1 O.C. "A" Company.
No. 2 O.C. "B"   "
No. 3 O.C. H.Q.   "
No. 4. File.
No. 5. War diary.

SECRET.   6th.Bn.London Regiment.   Copy No....
       OPERATION ORDER NO.28/1.

Reference O.O.28 dated 28/6/18.

In all cases read "D" Company for "A" Company except in para.3.

"A" Company will still supply working parties but these will report to Bn. H.Q. on their way up where guides will be met.

Relief must be complete by 10.0 p.m. and parties can be dribbles forward in small numbers.

Copies issued to :-

No.1. Commanding Officer.
No.2. O.C "A" Company.
No.3. O.C."B"   "
No.4. O.C."D" cc "
No.5. File.
No.6 War diary.

(sd) R.WYLIE. Capt.& Adjt.

SECRET.   6th. Bn. London Regiment.   Copy No..

app. I

WARNING ORDER.
No. 29.

29/6/18.

1. Battalion will relieve a battalion of 173rd. Infantry Bde on night of July 1/2nd as right battalion of Left Subsector of Divisional Front i.e., southern half of attached disposition map.

   "A" Company on right.
   "D"   "   " left.
   "B"   "   in support.
   "C"   "   " reserve.

2. Reconnaissance will take place tomorrow by Company Commanders who will report at Battn. H.Q. D.12.a.9.8 stating that they are to reconnoitre right battalion area. In case of error they should apply at Bn.H.Q. at D.12.a.8.8.

3. Acknowledge.

                                          (Sd) R. WYLIE Capt. & Adjt.

To. No.1 O.C. "A" Coy.
To. 2 O.C. "B" "
No. 3 O.C. "C" "
No. 4 O.C. "D" "
No. 5 O.C. H.Q. Details.
No. 6 Q.M. & T.O.

6 London Rgt Army Form C. 2118.
17/5/6

WAR DIARY
or
INTELLIGENCE SUMMARY.
(Erase heading not required.)

Vol 19
Page 1.

Place	Date	Hour	Summary of Events and Information	Remarks and references to Appendices
ALBERT. S.W. of	July 1918.			
	1.		Strength of Battalion — 44 Officers 816 O.Ranks.	Rks
			Present with Battalion — 24 " 660 "	Rks
			(excluding Battle Surplus)	
	1/2		Relieved 2/4th Bn London Regt in line, right Battalion, left sub-sector of Divisional front with two	App. I Rks
			companies in front line, one in support and one in reserve.	Rks
	2.		2 OR wounded	App II Rks
	3/4		Reserve Company returned left front company	Rks
	4		2 OR wounded	Rks
	5		2 OR wounded	
	5/6		Support Company relieved right front company	App III Rks
	6		1 OR wounded	Rks
	7/8.		Reserve company relieved left front company	App IV Rks
	9		23 reinforcements reported. 2nd Lt H. St J. HEWITT Killed.	Rks
	9/10		Relieved by 7th Bn London Rgt and moved into Brigade Reserve of left sub-sector of Divisional front	App V · Va Rks
			5 OR killed 5 OR wounded	Rks
	10		1 OR wounded	Rks

Army Form C. 2118.

WAR DIARY
INTELLIGENCE SUMMARY.
(Erase heading not required.)

Instructions regarding War Diaries and Intelligence Summaries are contained in F.S. Regs., Part II. and the Staff Manual respectively. Title pages will be prepared in manuscript.

Page 2.

Place	Date	Hour	Summary of Events and Information	Remarks and references to Appendices
ALBERT S.W. of	July 1918			
	12		2nd Lt J.S.R. LOVE and 72 OR joined for duty.	R15
	12/13		Relieved by 12th Bn. London Regt in 18th Division and moved to positions vacated by that unit in Divisional Reserve	App. VI & VIa R15
	15		Left Company BAZIEUX system relieved left company in LAVIEVILLE line (Div. Reserve)	R15
	18/19		Relieved 2/2nd Bn. London Regt in line, right sector of Divisional front, with three companies in line and one in support. One company of 1st Bn. 132nd American Regt attached, one platoon per company for instruction	App VII & VIIIa R15
	19/20		Company of 1st Bn. 132nd American Regt attached for instruction relieved by a company of 2nd Bn. 132nd American Regt.	R15
	21.		Major J.A. VENNING, 8th Bn. London Regt reported and assumed duties of Second in Command vice Major N.D. LUPTON who proceeded 20.7.1918 to take over duties as Commandant of 12th Divisional Reception Camp.	R15
	21/22		Company of 2nd Bn. 132nd American Regt relieved. Company of 3rd Bn. attached.	R15
	22.		2nd Lt J.S.R. LOVE, to Field Ambulance with accidentally cut knee.	R15
	23.		1 OR died of wounds. 1 OR wounded.	R15
	23/24		Company of 3rd Bn. 132nd American Regt relieved 115 unit	R15

WAR DIARY
INTELLIGENCE SUMMARY.
(Erase heading not required.)

Army Form C. 2118.

Page 3

Place	Date	Hour	Summary of Events and Information	Remarks and references to Appendices
	July 1918			
ALBERT S.W. of	23/24		Bn relieved in line by 1st Bn. 132nd American Regt and moved into support position	App. VIII & VIIIa Q.M.S
			relieved by 2/2nd Bn. London Regt.	
	25.		2nd Lt and Asst Adjt. C.H.L. BUBB to Field Amb. sick	Q.M.S
			1 O.R. wounded	Q.M.S
	26.			
	27/28		Relieved 1st Bn. 132nd American Regt in right subsector	App. IX & IXa Q.M.S
			2nd Lt N.S. MIDSON M.C. wounded at duty	Q.M.S
			1 O.R. killed	Q.M.S
	30/31.		Relieved in line by 2/10th Bn London Regt and moved into Divisional Reserve.	App. X Q.M.S

Royle
Captain and Adjutant.

SECRET. OPERATION ORDER Copy No. app I
           No. 30   3/7/18.
       8th. Bn. London Regiment.

1. "C" Company will relieve "D" Company on left company front tonight.

2. Reconnaissance and checking of stores will be carried out immediately. Details of relief to be arranged between company commanders.

3. All trench stores will be carefully taken over and handed over and receipts forwarded to this office immediately after relief.

4. In order not to interfere with working parties "C" Coy when proceeding up to relieve will take full kit etc and "D" Company on relief will dump packs and carry out working parties as per orders to be issued later. On completion of same, "D" Coy will collect packs and move back to new position. "C" Company will bring up all tools necessary for work by "D" Company. These tools will form part of trench stores taken over by "D" Company from "C" Company.

5. Completion of relief will be reported by Company Commanders name.

6. Acknowledge.

                              (sd) R. WYLIE. Capt. & Adjt.

app. IV

SECRET.   6th., Bn. London Regiment.   Copy No.

OPERATION ORDER   5/7/18.
No. 31.

1. "B" Company will relieve "A" Company on right company front tonight.

2. Reconnaissance and checking of stores will be carried out immediately. Details of relief wixx to be arranged between company commanders.

3. All trench stores will be carefully taken over and handed over and receipts forwarded to this office immediately after relief.

4. In order not to interfere with working parties "B" Coy when proceeding up to relieve will take full kit etc and "A" Coy on relief will dump packs and carry out working parties as per orders to be issued later. On completion of same, "A" Company will collect packs and move back to new position.

5. Completion of relief will be reported by Company Commanders name.

6. Acknowledge.

(Sd) R. WYLIE Capt. & Adjt.

SECRET.   OPERATION ORDER   Copy No..
                           No. 51
                    6th. Bn. London Regiment.   7/7/18.

1. "D" Coy will relieve "C" Coy on left company front tonight.

2. Reconnaissance and checking of stores will be carried out immediately. Details of relief to be arranged between Company Commanders.

3. O.C. "C" Coy will note that dispositions of "D" Coy have been altered.

4. All trench stores will be carefully taken over and handed over and receipts forwarded to this office immediately after relief.

5. In order not to interfere with working parties, "D" Coy when proceeding up to relieve will take full kit etc, and "C" Coy on relief will dump packs and carry out working parties as per orders to be issued later. On completion of same "C" Coy will collect packs and move back to new position. "D" Company will bring up all tools necessary for work by "C" Coy.

6. Completion of relief will be reported by Company Commander's name.

7. Acknowledge.

                                        (sd) R. WYLIE Capt. & Adjt.

App. IV

SECRET.   6th., Bn.London Regiment.   Copy No.

OPERATION ORDER NO. 32.

Map Sheet. SENLIS.

1. The 7th.Bn.London Regiment will relieve 6th.Bn.London Regiment on the right subsector on night 9/10th.July.

2. On completion of relief the 6th.Bn. will move back and take up position of battalion in Brigade Reserve.

3. Each company will detail an officer to proceed to H.Q. of the battalion in Brigade Reserve at D.5.d.25.30 to reconnoitre line to be taken up.

    "A" Coy to be on RIGHT.
    "C" "   " " in CENTRE.
    "D" "   " " on LEFT.
    "B" "   " " in RESERVE.

4. Completion of reconnaissance will be reported to this office not later than 6 p.m. this evening.

5. Further orders will be issued later.

6. Acknowledge.

                                    (sd) R.WYLIE Capt.& Adjt.

App Va

SECRET. 6th., Bn. London Regiment. Copy No...
9/7/18.

OPERATION ORDER
No. 33.

1. The battalion will be relieved by 7th.Bn.London Regiment tonight.

2. Order of relief :-

    "A" Coy 7th.Bn. relieves "B" Coy 6th.Bn.
    "D" "   "   "   "D" "   "
    "B" "   "   "   "A" "   "
    "C" "   "   "   "C" "   "

    Companies of 7th.Bn.London Regiment will relieve in following order:-
    "A" Coy - "D" Coy - "B" Coy - "C" Coy.

3. Guides. One guide per platoon and one for C.,H.Q. will report at these H.Qrs. not later than 9.45 p.m.

4. All trench stores will be carefully handed over and receipts obtained. These will be forwarded to this office by 8.0 a.m. on 10th.inst.

5. Empty petrol tins will be dumped at ration dump by 10.0 p.m. at the latest.

6. Sickles, whetstones and scythes as detailed will be placed on ration dump by 10.15 p.m.

7. Lewis Guns, drums and regimental trench stores will be carried out. Certificate will be rendered by midday tomorrow that guns and drums are complete.

8. Work in progress will be carefully handed over in detail.

9. Mess boxes, medical equipment, etc will be ready to be loaded by 10.30 p.m. at Bn.H.Q.Dump.

10. Code word for completion of this relief will be Company Commanders name.

11. On completion of this relief companies will move off independently to line vacated by 7th.Bn.

12. Advance party has already proceeded to take over stores. Copies of receipts given will be sent to new Bn.H.Q. by 10.0 a.m.

13. Distance of 200 yards will be maintained between platoons on the move.

14. At each relief photographs and maps useful for the front will be handed over. Work in progress will be carefully taken over in detail.

15. Rations will arrive in new area about 1.0 a.m. Watercart will go round each company to fill up all petrol tins at this time. All petrol tins must be at Company Dumps.

16. Code for arrival in new line will be "DONE" followed by Company Commander's name.

Distribution.   (Sd) R.WYLIE Capt.& Adjt.
No.1 Commanding Officer.
 "2/5 O.C.All Coy.
 " 6 O.C.,H.Q.Details.
 " 7 O.C., 7th.Bn.
 " 8 T.O.& Q.M.
 " 9 War Diary.

SECRET.   6th., Bn. London Regiment.   Copy No.

WARNING ORDER NO. 34   11/7/18.

1. This battalion will be relieved on night of 12/13th. July 1918 and will move to take up position in LAVIEVILLE Right Sector, i.e., the system occupied before the battalion moved up.
Order in line will be :-

    "A" Coy on right   ) LAVIEVILLE LINE.
    "C" "   " left   )

    "B" Coy on right   ) BAZIEUX LINE.
    "D" "   " left   )

H.Q. will be in BAZIEUX.

2. Usual taking over parties of 1 officer per company 1 N.C.O. per platoon and reliable N.C.O. from H.Q. will proceed to new area arriving not later than 10.0 a.m. on morning of 12th. inst.

3. Further instructions will be issued later.

4. Acknowledge.   (Sd) R. WYLIE Capt. & Adjt.

No.1 Commanding Officer.
 "2/5 Os.C. Companies
No.6 O.C.H.Q. Details.
 " 7 Q.M. & T.O.
8/9 War Diary.
No.10 File.

SECRET. 6th., Bn. London Regiment.   Copy No...

OPERATION ORDER   12/7/18.
No. 34.

Map Sheet. SENLIS.

1. The battalion will be relieved by 12th. Bn. London Regiment tonight.

2. Company reliefs will be as follows :-

   "B" Coy 12th. Bn. relieves "A" Coy 6th. Bn.
   "C"   "   "   "   "B"   "   "
   "D"   "   "   "   "C"   "   "
   "A"   "   "   "   "D"   "   "

3. Guides. One guide per platoon and one for Coy. H.Q. will be at track junction, D.11.a.4.4 at 10.15 p.m. L/Cp. Baker will be at this point and guides will report to him.

4. All trench stores will be carefully handed over with exception of regimental trench stores and receipts taken. These receipts will be forwarded to Battn. H.Q. by 10 a.m. 13/7/18.

5. Mess boxes will be dumped at Bn. H.Q. by 10 a.m.

6. Dixies etc will be dumped at Bn. H.Q. by 10 a.m. and guard will be left over them until collected by the transport.

7. Completion of relief will be notified by Company Commander's name.

8. Trenches will be left clean and tidy.

9. On completion of relief, companies will move off independantly to LAVIEVILLE Right sector as detailed in Warning Order No. 34, para.1   Bn. H.Q. will be at D.9.b.6.6.

10. All Lewis Guns and drums will be carried.

11. All Defence schemes and "Work in hand" schemes will be carefully handed and taken over.

12. Arrival in new area will be notified by Code Word "ARRIVED" followed by Company Commander's name.

13. Acknowledge.

(sd) R. WYLIE Capt. & Adjt.

Distribution :-
No. 1 Commanding Officer.
 " 2/5 O.C. All Coys.
 " 6 O.C., H.Q. Details.
 " 7 O.C. 12th. Bn. London Regiment.
 " 8 Q.M. & T.O.
 " 9/10 War Diary.
 " 11. File

SECRET. 6th.Bn., London Regiment Copy No.....

WARNING ORDER NO.36.

App VII

Map sheet. SENLIS.

1. The 6th.Bn.London Regiment will relieve 2/2nd.Bn.London Regt in the right subsection of the right sector on night 18/19th.July 1918, i.e, sector originally taken over from 15th.Bn.London Regiment.

2. As far as it is at present known, dispositions will be:-

    "B" Coy.   LEFT.
    "D" "   CENTRE.
    "C" "   RIGHT.
    "A" "   SUPPORT.

3. O.C.Coys will reconnoitre early tomorrow morning and will also send parties consisting of one officer per company, one N.C.O. per platoon and one reliable sergeant sergeant from H.Q. to take over trench stores. These parties will remain until arrival of battalion.

4. Defence schemes, maps, aeroplane photographs, etc, etc., and trench stores will be carefully checked and taken over.

5. Copies of receipts for trench stores etc will be forwarded to new Bn.H.Q. by 10 a.m. 19th.inst.

6. American platoons attached to British Companies will be taken over by relieving companies.

7. Overcoats, haversacks and caps of "C" & "D" Coys will be on company dumps at 11 a.m. tomorrow. Overcoats will be properly tied in bundles of ten and labelled. C.Q.M.Sgts will supervise this work.

8. Overcoats, haversacks and caps of "A" & "B" Coys will be on company dumps by 10 p.m. properly tied and labelled as above.

9. Further instructions will be issued later.

10. Acknowledge.

(Sd) R.WYLIE Captain & Adjutant.

Issued to :-
No.1 Commanding Officer.
 "2/5 O.C.All Coys.
 " 6 O.C., H.Q.Details.
 " 7 O.C.2/2nd.London Regiment.
 " 8 Q.M.& T.O.
 " 9 File
 " 10 War Diary.
 " 11   "

SECRET.   6th. Bn. London Regiment.   Copy No.
                                                18/7/18.
                    OPERATION ORDER
                        No. 36.

Map. SENLIS. Reference Warning Order No.36 dated 18/7/18.

1.   "C" Coy 6th.Bn. relieves "C" Coy 2/2nd.Bn. on right.
        "D" "   "   "   "B" "   "   in centre.
        "B" "   "   "   "D" "   "   on left.
        "A" "   "   "   "A" "   "   in support.

2.   Companies will relieve in the following order :-

        6th.Bn. - "C" - "D" - "B" - "A" - H.Q.

3.   Guides. will be met at junction of LAVIEVILLE track and AMIENS-
        ALBERT ROAD one per platoon in charge of Intelligence Officer
        of 2/2nd.Bn. at D.16.d.5.8.

4.   Platoons will move at distance of 200 yards - first platoon
        of "C" Coy to be at this point at 10.0 p.m.

5.   All trench stores in present sector, maps, photographs etc,
        etc., will be carefully handed over and receipts obtained and
        forwarded to Bn.H.Q. by 10.0 a.m.

6.   All Lewis Guns and 24 drums per gun will be carried.
        Remainder of drums to be dumped on company dump by 10 p.m.
        also dixies etc.

7.   Guard will be left on all stores dumped by each company,
        until same have been collected by transport when each guard
        will report to its own company in new position.

8.   Water and rations will arrive at new company dump about 1 a.m.
        and will be carried forward to the three front companies by
        company parties.

9.   One platoon of the American battalion will be taken over
        by each company of this unit for rations, water and accommodation.

10.   Six S.O.S. rockets per company and eight for Bn.H.Q. will
        be taken over.

11.   Tommy cookers at rate of 35 per company will be issued
        tonight.

12.   Company A.A.guns posts will be taken over companies until
        further instructions are issued. H.Q. will mount two A.A.Guns.

13.   Trenches are to be left clean and tidy.

14.   Completion of relief will be reported to new Bn.H.Q. by
        Company Commanders. name.

15.   Acknowledge.

                            (sd) R.WYLIE Captain & Adjutant.

Issued to recipients of W.O.36.

SECRET.　　　　6th., Bn. London Regiment.　　Copy No..
　　　　　　　　　OPERATION ORDER NO. 37.　　　23/7/18.
Map Sheet.
SENLIS.

1. This battalion will be relieved tonight by the 1st. Bn. 132nd. American Regiment.

2. **Guides.** One guide per platoon, one per Coy.H.Q. and two for Bn.H.Q. will be at a place to be notified later by 10 p.m.

3. Relief will be in following order :-

    1. Centre Company.
    2. Left Company.
    3. Support Company.
    4. Right Company.

4. (a) Relief for "D" Coy will proceed up DUKE ST Left front platoon and support platoons will go out via DOG TRENCH (and DOLLY) on to the track down from C.C.S. and thence down track past Bn,H.Q.
Right platoon will go out via road under bank at the C.C.S. thence as above.

  (b) Relief for B Company will enter via DUKE STREET.
    B Company will leave via ECHUCA ALLEY.

  (c) A Company relief will enter via DIAMOND LANE.
    A Company will leave straight back over the top.

  (d) C Company relief for front line platoons will come in via road through C.C.S. For Support platoon to DOLLY TRENCH via WELCH TRENCH.
    For Reserve platoon via Southern track i.e., track on right of Right platoon to WELCH TRENCH.

    C Company will go out as follows :-
    Front line platoon via C.C.S. track.
    Support platoon via C.C.S. track.
    Reserve platoons via WELCH TRENCH and Southern track.

5. All Lewis Guns and drums will be carried out and certificate will be rendered by noon 24/7/18 that these are complete.

6. Statement re petrol tins has been sent to companies shewing numbers to be handed over to incoming unit and numbers to be returned by transport. All empty tins will however be dumped on company dumps by 10 p.m. in separate stacks and a guard with full knowledge of what is to be with each stack will be left in charge.

7. All sickles, sythes and whetstones and any other stores to be taken out will be on company dumps at 10 p.m.

8. Food containers, Orderly Room Box, dixies, etc, etc., will be on road by Bn.H.Q. for removal at 10 p.m.

9. Maltese cart will report to R.A.P. about 10.30 p.m.

10. All trench stores, artillery maps, statement of work in hand, etc, etc., will be carefully handed over and receipts obtained in duplicate which will be forwarded to this office by noon tomorrow.

11. Trenches will be left clean and tidy, and latrine buckets etc properly emptied.

12. When relieving, companies will hand over foring positions etc and available accommodation and will not remain to attempt to find accommodation for the whole of the incoming unit.

25/7/18.

SECRET.   ADDENDA No.1 to OPERATION ORDER NO.37

Reference para.3.

A Company 6th.Bn. will be relieved by C Coy American Regt.
B   "   "   "   "   "   "   A "   "   "
C   "   "   "   "   "   "   D "   "   "
D   "   "   "   "   "   "   B "   "   "

Reference para.2.

Guides will report at Bn.H.Q. at 3.0 p.m. carrying unexpended portion of day's rations.

(sd) R.WYLIE Captain & Adjt.

Issued to :-
Recipients of O.O.37.

App VIII a

SECRET.   6th., Bn. London Regiment.   Copy No.
                                                 23/7/18.
                    OPERATION   ORDER
                        No. 37a.

Map Sheet. SENLIS.

1. On completion of relief as detailed in O.O.37 this battalion will relieve 2/2nd. Bn. London Regiment in Brigade Reserve with H.Q. at D.17.b.

2. Order of relief :-
    A Company 6th. Bn. will relieve D Coy. 2/2nd. Bn.
    B   "   "   "   "   A   "   "
    C   "   "   "   "   B   "   "
    D   "   "   "   "   B   "   "

3. One officer per company, N.C.O. per platoon, one N.C.O. per Bn.H.Q. and one guide per platoon who should have previously studied the routes taken by this unit on relief from the line, will report at this office at 4.0 p.m. today. They will then proceed to new Bn.H.Q. where guides will be supplied to take them to new company positions.
    The officers and NCC.O.s will take over trench stores and remain in new position.
    Guides will reconnoitre routes so as to pick the most suitable in conjunction with the routes already laid down.

4. All trench stores will be carefully checked and taken over and receipts forwarded to this office by noon tomorrow.

5. Water for tonight is being sent up tonight by 2/2nd. Bn.

6. Location of ration dump will be notified as soon as possible. There will be a watercart near Bn.H.Q.

7. Rations for tomorrow will be taken to new position.

8. Completion of relief will be notified by code word "THIRD".

9. Acknowledge.

                        (Sd)   R. WYLIE Captain & Adjutant.

Copies to
Recipients of O.O.37.

SECRET.   6th. Bn. London Regiment.   Copy No..
26/7/18.
WARNING ORDER NO. 38.

Map Sheet.   ******************************
SENLIS.

1. The 6th. Bn. London Regiment will relieve 1st. Bn. 132nd. American Regiment in the right subsector of the right sector on night 27/28 July 1918.

2. Positions of the companies will be ;-

   "A" Company on Right.
   "B"   "   in Centre.
   "D"   "   on left.
   "C"   "   in Support.

3. Company Commanders will reconnoitre new line early tomorrow morning.

4. One officer per company, 1 N.C.O. per platoon and one reliable N.C.O. per H.Q. will also proceed to new position to take over trench stores etc. These parties will remain until arrival of battalion.

5. Defence schemes, maps, aeroplane photographs, etc, etc., and trench stores will be carefully checked and taken over.

6. Copies of receipts given will be forwarded to Bn. H.Q. by 10 am. 23/7/18.

7. Lewis Guns and magazines will be carried.

8. Dixies and other stores not for line will be on company dumps by 10 p.m.

9. Further instructions will be issued.

10. Acknowledge.

(sd) R. WYLIE Capt & Adjt.

SECRET.   6th.Bn., London Regiment.   Copy No..

OPERATION ORDER
No.39.

Map sheet. SENLIS.

1. Further to WarningOrder No.38 dated 26/7/18:

    A Coy 6th.Bn. relieves D Coy 1st.Bn. 132nd.American Regt.
    B "   "   "   B "   "   "   "
    C "   "   "   A "   "   "   "
    D "   "   "   C "   "   "   "

2. Relief will be in following order :-

    6th.Bn. 1st.Left Coy   (D Coy).
             2nd.Centre Coy (B Coy).
             3rd.Right Coy (A Coy).
             4th.Support Coy (C Coy).

3. D Coy will enter via DUKE ST, DOLLY TRENCH and ECHUCA ALLEY Americans leave via ECHUCA ALLEY.

    B Coy will enter via DUKE ST into EMU and DOLLY TRENCH southern part of company to be relieved will lead out via C.C.S. and northern via DUKE ST.

    A Coy will enter by track (C.C.S) into WELCH, DOLLY and EMU etc.

    Americans will leave via same track.

    C Coy will enter over the top and if necessary via DIAMOND LANE.

    Americans will leave by same route.

4. <u>Guides</u>. One guide per platoon and one for Coy H.Q. will be at new Bn.H.Q. by 10 p.m. If the night is dark, companies will proceed at 10 p.m. and if moonlight not until 10.30 p.m.
    Further instructions re this time will be issued.

5. 200 yards distance between platoons will be maintained.

6. Separate instructions have been issued to the Transport Officer.

7. Instructions re petrol tins in this sector have been issued separately.

8. Rations for consumption tomorrow will arrive in new position by 1 a.m.

9. Completion of relief will be reported by code word "FORTY"

10. Instructions regarding relief of this battalion by the 7th.Bn. in this position will be issued this afternoon.

11. Acknowledge.

                            (sd) R.WYLIE. Capt.& Adjt.
Issued to Recipients of O.O.38.

SECRET.   6th.Bn., London Regiment.   Copy No.

ADDENDA No.1   27/7/18.
TO OPERATION ORDER NO.39.

1. This battalion will be relieved by 7th.Bn.London Regiment in this sector this evening.

2. As it will be impossible to wait for the 7th.Bn., parties from the latter battalion are being sent in advance to take over stores and to act as guides and guards. Companies will therefore vacate their present positions as per O.O.39 and according to orders to be issued later.

3. Each company will leave a guard on property and stores at company dumps until this has been cleared by 6th.Bn. transport. These guards will report to new Bn.H.Q. where they will be sent up to rejoin their respective companies.

4. All trench stores, maps, defence schemes and amendments and bath- guard and Stragglers Post will be carefully handed over and receipts obtained for former. These receipts will be handed in to Orderly Room by 10 a.m. tomorrow.

5. Acknowledge.

(sd) R.WYLIE. Capt.& Adjt.

Issued to All recipients of OO.39.

13. Companies will carefully reconnoitre the routes to be taken on relief, as far as a line drawn approximately N and S through Bn.H.Q.

14. Further instructions as to xx other guides to learn routes to new position will be issued as soon as possible.

15. One officer per company will be detailed to remain behind for 24 hours with the incoming unit.

16. Completion of relief will be reported to this office by code word SECOND.

17. Acknowledge.

(sd) R.WYLIE Captain & Adjutant.

Copies issued to :-
No. 1 Commanding Officer.
" 2/5 O.C.Companies.
" 6 O.C.1st.Bn.132nd.Regt.
" 7 Q.M.& T.O.
" 8 O.C., H.Q.Details.
" 9 War Diary.
" 10 "
" 11 File.

"A" Form.
Army Form C. 2121.
(In pads of 100.)

MESSAGES AND SIGNALS.

No. of Message..............

Prefix........ Code....... Words. Charge.
Office of Origin and Service Instructions.

SECRET

Sent At.........m.
To.........
By.........

This message is on a/c of:

7

...........Service.
(Signature of "Franking Officer.")

Recd. at.........m.
Date.........
From.........
By.........

TO HQ 174th Infantry Brigade

Sender's Number. Day of Month. In reply to Number. AAA
~~QU155~~ WD.6   1

Enclosed please find War Diary and Appendices for month of May 1918.

From 6th Bn. Lond Regt
Place
Time

The above may be forwarded as now corrected. (Z) JHLB... 2/11/May
Censor. Signature of Addressor or person authorized.

* This line should be erased if not required.

174th Bde.
────────

58th Div.
────────

6th BATTALION

LONDON REGIMENT

AUGUST 1918

WAR DIARY
INTELLIGENCE SUMMARY.
(Erase heading not required.)

Army Form C. 2118.

6 London Regt

Page 1.

Place	Date	Hour	Summary of Events and Information	Remarks and references to Appendices
Maps Sheet. 62.D.N.E. 62.C.N.W.	August 1918.			
ROUND WOOD nr. CONTAY.	1.		In Divisional Reserve in ROUND WOOD	Pls
CANAPLES.	2.		Moved by march route and bus to CANAPLES and accommodated in billets.	Pls App. I.
	3.		Cleaning up, refitting, etc.	Pls
LAHOUSSOYE.	4/5		Moved by march route and bus to LAHOUSSOYE and accommodated in billets.	Pls App II
	5/6		Relieved Northants Regt in Support position. HQ situated at V.22.d.2.4.	Pls
	6.		Enemy attacked front line system S.W. of MORLANCOURT. Battalion stood to. 2nd Lt. H.E. HOPKINS to hospital sick.	Pls
			Casualties :- Officers - NIL 2 O.R. Killed 2 O.R. wounded.	Pls
	7.	10.20 p.m	Bn moved to assembly tapes. HQ moved to V.23.d.8.4.	Pls
			Casualties :- 2nd Lt. F.H. ABEL gassed. 3 O.R. Killed 3 O.R. wounded	Pls
	8.	4:20am	Bn attacked enemy's position. See Commanding Officer's report attached marked App III	App III Pls
	9.	4.20 pm	— do — — do — —	Pls
			Casualties total fr 8/9th August 1918. Lieut-Col. C.B. BENSON. D.S.O. Named at duty.	
			Capt. F. HILL. D.C.M. Killed. Capt. D.W. ANDERSON. M.C. Killed. 2nd Lt. H. SIMPSON.	
			Wounded :- Lieut. H.H. DUNN. 2nd Lt. G. Sr. V.R. CHORLTON. 2nd Lt. V.R. LOVE 2nd Lt. H. SIMPSON.	
			2nd Lt. R.N. DEARSLEY. 2nd Lt. H.N.C. NIGHTINGALE. 2nd Lt. A. SMITH. N.S. FOX.	
			O.Ranks. Killed 32. Wounded 243. Wounded at duty 4. Missing 24.	Pls

WAR DIARY
INTELLIGENCE SUMMARY.
(Erase heading not required.)

Army Form C. 2118.

Page 2.

Place	Date	Hour	Summary of Events and Information	Remarks and references to Appendices
	August 1918.			
	10		Bn was withdrawn and reorganized. HQ at N.33.d.5.4.	R/S
			50 O.R. under Major V. VENNING moved up to hold posts in N.34.b and d.	R/S
	11.		Early in morning the Bn was relieved by Australian troops and moved to accommodation in V.24.b. and d. with HQ at V.24.b.85.80.	R/S
ROUND WOOD	12/13		Resting and refitting	R/S
near CONTAY	13		Bn moved to and accommodated under canvas in ROUND WOOD.	R/S
	14.		Refitting and reorganising.	R/S
	15		Training, smartening up, attack formation, musketry, etc.	R/S
			2nd/Lt. P.J. FROST. J. TRIMM G.H. WILLCOCKS & 150 O.R. joined for duty.	
	16/17		Training etc as above	R/S
	17.		G.M. in Chief inspected Bn whilst at training.	R/S
	19/21		Training etc as above	R/S
	19.		2nd/Lt. G.P. TICKLE. T.N. MAPLE and 150 O.R. joined for duty.	R/S
	21.		2nd/Lt. C.W.B. FIELD and 22 O.R. joined for duty.	R/S
HEILLY.	22	5.55am	Bn moved by march route to neighbourhood of HEILLY (C.24.a.9.2.) with Battle Surplus and Jumpoff Lines at ROUND WOOD	App IV R/S

Army Form C. 2118.

WAR DIARY
INTELLIGENCE SUMMARY.
(Erase heading not required.)

Instructions regarding War Diaries and Intelligence
Summaries are contained in F. S. Regs., Part II.
and the Staff Manual respectively. Title pages
will be prepared in manuscript.

Page 3.

Place	Date	Hour	Summary of Events and Information	Remarks and references to Appendices
	August 1918.			
	23		Battle Surplus moved to MIRVAUX.	Pls.
			Lieut. Col. C.B. BENSON. D.S.O. proceeded on one month's leave.	Pls.
			Major J. VENNING assumed command of Bn.	
	23	8.0 am	Bn moved by march route to D.17.a and c. DARWIN COPSE and arrived at 10.30 a.m.	Pls.
	24	6.0 am	- do - K.13.a.5.4. - do - 9.0 am	Pls.
	25	2.0 am	- do - K.10.d.5.4 - do - 3.50 a.m.	Pls.
		8.30 am	- do - L.2.a.50.15 - do - 10.35 am	Pls.
		6.0 pm	Bn proceeded in artillery formation as support Bn to 7th Bn 8th Bro Lond Rgt & took up position in F.29.c. and L.S.a.	Pls.
			Transport lines moved to MERICOURT L'ABBE.	
	26	5.15 am	Bn proceeded to L.b.a. 47 Casualties:- OR 31 OR killed 27 wounded	Pls.
			Capt. E.C.GREEN and 2nd/Lt L.J. GREGORY - wounded 1 missing 1 wounded at duty	Pls.
		noon.	Two companies start to to support line Relvd by 7th & 8th Bns London Rgt.	Pls.
	26/7	midnight	Bn moved forward to place of assembly for attack	Pls.
	27	4.55am	Bn attacked and gained objective with HQ at A.29.a.7.4 See report by Commanding Officer attached marked app. V	App V. Pls
	28	4.55am	Attack continued and objectives gained	
	29/4.		Relieved by 12th Bn London Rgt and retired into reserve.	

Army Form C. 2118.

WAR DIARY
INTELLIGENCE SUMMARY.
(Erase heading not required.)

Page 4.

Place	Date	Hour	Summary of Events and Information	Remarks and references to Appendices
	August 1918			
			Total casualties during operations 28/29th August 1918:-	
			Killed:- 2/Lt. W.E.C. WHITE. Wounded:- Capt B. BURT- SMITH. M.C. Lieut. E. C.	RJS
			WHITWORTH. 2nd Lts. J.E. ROSE. A.J.W. FROST. L.C. LEAPMAN. G.P. TICKLE.	RJS
			G.H. WILLCOCKS. Capt/adj: R. WYLIE. - sick to Hospital.	RJS
			O.Ranks.	RJS
	28		Transport lines moved to 1 kilo N. from BRAY-SUR-SOMME	
	30		Bn. proceeded by march route and bus to B.23.d.	
	31	4.30 am	Bn. assembled for attack on "HARRIERES" WOOD, attacking at 5.10 am. Objectives were gained	App VI
			— see Commanding Officers report attached marked "App VI"	RJS
			Transport lines to SPUR WOOD.	
			Casualties during operations 31st August 1918:-	
	31		Killed:- 2nd Lt. W.D. SOULSBY. Wounded Lieut. J.V. BALL. 2/Lt. E.J. WOODHAMS. and	RJS
			2/Lt. L. HARBOTT (7th Bn. Lond Regt temporarily att'chd)	RJS
			O.Ranks:- Killed - 11. Wounded - 60 O.Ranks.	RJS
			Strength of unit. 24 Officers. Missing - 13.	RJS
			Nos. present. 11 " 532 "	

R.J.Taylor
Lt. Captain and Adjutant.
16th Bn. London Regiment.

SECRET.
8th Bn, London Regiment.
Operation Order
No 41.

Copy No.
17/8/1918.

app. 1

Maps, sheet
62D.
LENS.
AMIENS.

1. The battalion will move from present area tomorrow by bus and march route, will attend a tank demonstration and will probably arrive at CANAPLES at about 8.0 pm.

2. The battalion will move by march route to the S. edge of AGNICOURT on the BEHENCOURT – AGNICOURT Road in following order:-
   A Coy   B Coy   C Coy   D Coy   H.Q.
   One hundred yards distance between platoons will be maintained.

3. Dress. Full marching order. Caps will be carried in haversacks and will only be worn on the order being given by the Commanding Officer

4. Starting point. Northern edge of wood. Leading company pass the starting point at 7.30 am.

5. Battalion will debuss one mile S.E. of ST. VAAST EN CHAUSSEE on the AMIENS – ST VAAST ROAD and will attend demonstration VAUX en AMIENOIS. At the conclusion of this the battalion will proceed by march route to CANAPLES.

6. Lewis Guns will be carried to embussing point and will be taken on busses for the demonstration. Two limbers will be provided to take these guns to CANAPLES on conclusion of the demonstration.

7. All drums & spare parts bags will be labelled and stacked on Northern entrance of the track to wood (on West side) by 5.15 am. Officers valises, Orderly Room boxes will be at same place at same time. This is the latest possible time for dumping.

8. The Medical cart will be loaded up at the R.A.P. at the same time.

9. Officers' Mess boxes will be outside guard tent at 7.15am at latest.

10. Breakfast – 5.15 am. (Cookers must be clear by 6.0 am)
    Rations for mid-day meal will be served out before departure and a meal will be provided on arrival at CANAPLES.

11. Waterbottles will be filled before departure. Watercarts will leave about 6.15 am.

12. Mens' packs will be left in the busses at debussing point and will be taken to dumping point near CANAPLES from whence they will be transported under Battalion arrangements.

13. C.Q.M.Sgts and two men per bus, preferably elderly men or light duty men from Details who are joining the battalion tonight will accompany the busses and will not debus at the point above named. The senior C.Q.M.Sgt will notify the Transport Officer at CANAPLES the exact location of the dump so formed.

14. 2/Lt. N.S.Kidson, M.G. will act as embussing officer and will report at embussing point at 8.0 am taking with him detailed statement of Bn.

15. Separate instructions have been issued to the Transport Officer.

16. The Camp will be left clean and tidy. OC.Coys are responsible for their own area.

17. Acknowledge.

R. Boyle
Captain and Adjutant.

SECRET.   6th. Bn. London Regiment.   Copy No........

                         WARNING ORDER No.41.
                         ====================

1.   The battalion will move from present area this evening by
bus and march route.

2.   Starting Point:- "D" Coys H.Qrs.
        Companies will move in the following order :-

             D Coy - B Coy - A Coy - C Coy - H.Q.Coy.

        100 yards distance will be maintained between companies.

3.   Route :- CANAPLES - HAVERNES Rd where busses will be stationed.

4.   First company will pass starting point 7.30 p.m.

5.   Dress. Full marching order unless otherwise ordered.

6.   Companies will be told off in parties of 25 for each bus.

7.   Brigade Embussing Officer :- 2/ Lieut. W.S.Kirson M.C.

8.   The Battalion Embussing Officer will be 2/Lieut.H.E.Hopkins.
This officer will report to Brigade Embussing Officer at
embussing point at the N.W. edge of HAVERNES on the HAVERNES -
CANAPLES Rd at 8.30 p.m. and will take with him embussing
embussing states. He will report to Battalion Orderly Room
for further instructions before departure.

9.   All Lewis Guns and 24 drums per gun will be carried.

10.   Rations for tomorrow's consumption will be issued this
afternoon, and carried on the man.

11.   Officers valises will be at Q.M.Stores by 4 p.m. Mess boxes
will be at H.Q.Mess by 6 p.m. Orderly Room boxes at Bn.H.Qrs
by 4 p.m. unless otherwise ordered.

12.   Billets will be left clean and tidy and a certificate to
this effect will be handed into Orderly Room by 7 p.m.

13.   ACKNOWLEDGE.

                              (Sd) R.WYLIE   Captain & Adjutant.

Copies issued to :-

No.1 Commanding Officer.
No.2 Second-in-Command.
No.3/6 O.C.All Coys.
No.7 O.C., H.Q.Details.
No.8 Q.M.& T.O.
No.9 War Diary.
No.10 File.

App. III

REPORT ON OPERATIONS; 6th. Bn. LONDON REGIMENT.

8th. & 9th. AUGUST 1918.

OBJECTIVES.

The objective allotted to the battalion was the GREEN LINE, extending from the SOMME in K.33.d to just E of the junction of the Wood and track in K.27-d.7.4.
Two companies were to take this line by making for the N end of MALARD WOOD and then swinging down southward under cover of the barrage, seize the line.
A third was to work around the south of MALARD WOOD, join up with the Northern Companies, and watch the right flank.
The fourth company and one company of 8th. Bn. London Regiment, were to consolidate on the West side of MALARD WOOD and thus form a second line.

TAPE LINE ASSEMBLY.

The battalion was to assemble on a taped line in K25.a.&c in the following order from right to left, A.Coy-D.Coy with one company of 8th. Bn. London Regiment- C.Coy with B.Coy behind them- two companies 7th. Bn. London Regiment supported by one company 7th. Bn. London Regt. behind them.
The L.T.Ms. and M.Gs. behind the units to which they are allotted
Troops were to be on the taped line two hours before ZERO.

BARRAGE.

The barrage line ran from N.E. to S.W. and was to cover the advance to beyond the GREEN LINE where it was to halt for one hour to cover the consolidation and give the 173rd. Brigade time to close with it preparatory to starting for their objectives.

TANKS.

Tanks were allotted to proceed with the infantry. Of these the following were to directly help this battalion viz:-
4 to proceed round N of MALARD WOOD and operate in K27d and K35b.
1 to K27c.
1 to accompany infantry S of MALARD WOOD.
1 to go through SAILLY-LAURETTE and along the road from this village to CHIPILLY.

TERRAIN.

The ground to be crossed has its features running from N.E. to S.W. All roads, valleys and woods had this trend. This together with the barrage line which coincided with these features, tended to draw advancing troops southwards.

NARRATIVE OF EVENTS.

The battalion moves off for its assembly position at 10.20p.m. on 7th.instant. It was estimated that four hours would be required to get the battalion on the tape line. This proved to be correct. Two companies who had been cut in half by elements of 173rd. Brigade arrived late and only got on the tape shortly before ZERO.

It was a clear morning until shortly before 4a.m. when a heavy mist fell. At zero hour the battalion was on the tape with Bn.H.Q. at J23d.8.4.-connected to Brigade H.Q. by telephone. The Battalion Command Post was at J19c 4.0 connected with Battalion by telephone.

A few casualties from shell fire and machine guns occured on the tape line, but generally the troops formed up practically unmolested.

The barrage came down at 4.20a.m. and the line advanced in good order into the thick mist, through which one could not see more than 20 yards. The TANKS were not with the infantry at this time.

The barrage appeared to be very good, and the troops losing sense of direction owing to the mist, followed it. The enemy put up a resistance in their front line, but this was soon overcome and prisoners immediately started coming in in considerable numbers.

Before going any great distance companies and battalions became mixed except on the extreme right flank, and the general of the attack was S.E.

There was little resistance except on the right flank where they had to fight their way forward practically from the QUARRY in K.31d 7.8. to the high ground in K.33.b. The right flank was greatly assisted by a TANK coming from the direction of SAILLY-LAURETTE.

On the mist beginning to lift a composite company formed from stragglers and prisoners guards was sent forward under the Intelligence Officer to support the right flank.

The position at 10a.m. appeared to be as follows:-
7th.Bn. London Regt. partly at their objectives.
A party of 6th.Bn. London Regt. at QUARRY E of MALARD WOOD.
W edge of MALARD WOOD held by elements of 6th-7th & 8th.Bns. London Regt. and 173rd Brigade.
Machine Guns in position on W of MALARD WOOD.
No touch established between 6th and 7th.Bns. London Regiment on E side of WOOD.

Although the wood seemed to be practically free of the enemy it did not appear to be occupied by out troops. The following dispositions were therefore made:-

(1) A party of about 3 Officers and 60 O.R. of the 8th.Bn, London Regt. were dispatched to reinforce the 7th.Bn. London Regt. on the left flank.

(2) A Company of 6th.Bn. London Regt. that had just been reorganised was despatched to secure and hold the high ground S of MALARD WOOD, and connect Northwards along E side of MALARD WOOD with the 7th.Bn.London Regt.

(3) The composite company, under the Intelligence Officer, to hold the high ground in K.32b and cover the company advancing to high ground S of MALARD WOOD.

(4) A request of O.C.2/2nd.London Regt to push two companies straight through MALARD WOOD from W to E and make it secure.
(Note; the O.C.2/2nd.London Regt states that he had already despatched two companies for this purpose).

The wood was secured without difficulty, but units of 174th.Brigade and 173rd.Brigade were considerably mixed and the line was reorganised as follows:-

(1) Men of the 7th.Bn.London Regt. were despatched to rejoin their own unit.

(2) Men of 18th.Division were despatched to Battalion H.Q.

(3) Men of the 8th.Bn.London Regt. retained.

(4) A Company Commander of 2/3rd.Bn. London Regt. instructed to take over posts on E side of MALARD WOOD from 6th.Bn.London Regt. with men of his own battalion.

(5) 6th.Bn.London Regt. to hold support Line on W side of MALARD WOOD.

Before this reorganisation was completed the 173rd. Brigade attacked. As no nitification of this attack had been received, no steps were taken to relieve elements of 173rd. Brigade on E side of WOOD.
The consequence was that a gap was created between the un-relieved posts of the 6th.Bn.London Regt. about K35 Central, and 7th. Bn. London Regt. The gap was filled by those of 183rd. Brigade who failed to get forward, but principally by 9th.Bn.London Regt.
MALARD WOOD was thus more than sufficiently held for night of 8/9th August.

Headquarters of Battalions of 174th. Brigade were at this time as follows:-

    6th. Battalion ... ... K.31.b.2.7.
    7th. Battalion ... ... K.25.d.9.8.
    8th. Battalion ... ... K.26.c.3.5.

OPERATIONS OF 9th. AUGUST 1918 :- near CHIPILLY.

At about 2.15p.m. on 9th. August orders were received to take the CHIPILLY RIDGE, that three TANKS and four machine were allotted, that CHIPILLY was reported clear by the Australians, and that there would be no Artillery Barrage.

The strength of the battalion less Bn. H.Q. and four officers and 160 O.R.

The objective was roughly the track on CHIPILLY RIDGE running N.W. from K.35.a.9.5. to K.34.b.9.5. facing N.E.

The scheme for the attack was as follows:-

One Tank to work through CHIPILLY around the S of the ridge and thence northwards by the raod in the valley and E of CHIPILLY RIDGE.

One Tank to proceed up the ridge by raod running N.E. through K.34.d and K.35.c.

One Tank to proceed northward along road in valley on W side of CHIPILLY RIDGE.

Infantry to form up on N & S line K.33.d.1.8. to K.33.b.15.00. behind the wood and advance with track running from K.33.b.15.00 to K.34.c4.8.as their boundary. On reaching the top bank on the ridge in K.34.d they were to advance with the road running N.E. up the ridge as their directing line, straight to their objective. Four machine guns were to follow them, two guns to protect the right flank, two to protect the left.

When the attack was ordered my men were partly in posts on S.E. corner of MALARD WOOD and partly in MALARD WOOD itself. The Intelligence Officer was at once sent forward to give the Officer Commanding the Battalion company a general idea of the scheme and to help to assemble the men. On this being done the details of the scheme was explained to the officers taking part, and the Zero hour fixed for 4.15p.m.

At this time there were posts of 9th.Bn.London Regiment in CELESTINES WOOD, running roughly K.33.b.5.0.-K.34.a.1.7.-K.28.c.10.00.

CHIPILLY was reported clear and CELESTINES WOOD was thought probably clear. Granted CHIPILLY and CELESTINES WOOD being clear it appeared only necessary to march on in artillery formation and occupy CHIPILLY RIDGE. As it did not appear probable however that these places were empty, orders were given to carefully watch the flanks, especially the right flank.

The TANKS and infantry advanced punctually at 4-15p.m. Directly the infantry debouched from the Eastern edge of the Wood in K.33.d they were met by extremely heavy machine gun fire from CHIPILLY RIDGE and from S.W. corner of CELESTINES WOOD. They suffered very heavy casualties and could make no headway. The machine guns were pushed up on their right flank to help them. Operations were in this state when the 10th.Bn. London Regiment appeared. The O.C. this battalion sent direct to my men and also commenced working towards CHIPILLY, where four hostile guns had been accounted for by a Tank,and thence Northwards up the ridge. My men were then withdrawn to K.33.b.6.0. were they met Americans. Lieut.Idris, who was in Command of the Battalion Company, assumed command of the Americans and the remnants of his company, worked someway N.E.through CELESTINS WOOD and then due E for the 85 contour on CHIPILLY RIDGE. This objective he successfully reached almost at the same time, but shortly the 10th.Bn.London Regiment, who had swept up the ridge from the south. Lieut.Idris fired his success signal and supervised the consolidation. Seeing that there were more than enough troops to hold the ridge Lieut.Idris handed over to the Americans and withdrew his very tired men to Battalion Headquarters at K.35.d.8.2. arriving there about 5a.m. on the 10th.inst.

One Tank had its "exhaust" pierced in CHIPILLY and had to return.
One Tank was burnt out at about K.34.c.55 evidently whilst trying to come to the help of the infantry.
What happened to the third Tank is not known.

CAPTURES.

A large number of prisoners and machine guns and mortars were captured by the battalion during the operatons, besides one .77 gun, two 4-2 Howitzers and one Heavy or medium trench mortar.

COMMUNITION.

Communition was kept up by telephone and runners with Brigade.
By runners with companies until the 10th.inst, when company headquarters was connected up with Battalion Headquarters by telephone

MEDICAL ARRANGEMENTS.

Company Stretcher Bearers accompanied Company Headquarters. Battalion stretcher Bearers moved forward at 10a.m. to search the ground for wounded. Many R.A.M.C. bearers were in COOTAMUNDRA STREET where they appeared to be absolutely useless.

FORMATIONS.

Formations for both attacks was two platoons of each company in front line followed at 25 yards distance by the remaining two platoons. The front line platoons advanced with one section extended to the front L.G. sections in two blocks on one flank, and the remaining rifle section in file on the other.

CASUALTIES.

12 Officers and 308 Other Ranks.

REMARKS.

WEATHER.

The mist which greatly helped operations in the initial stages, greatly hampered progress later. If it had lifted earlier I have no doubt that the Tanks would have been able to co-operate effectively and 173rd Brigade would have gained their objectives.

MEDICAL ARRANGEMENTS.

R.A.M.C. Stretcher Bearers remained to far behind. It is suggested that squads of about 20 should be attached to each battalion to be used by Battalion Commanders as required.

The O.C.s. is not sufficiently mobile, wounded cannot be got to it under 6 to 8 hours.

SUPPLY TANKS.

Supply Tanks are good, but each should carry one N.C.O., (C.Q.M.S. preferred) and one O.R. to guard supplies when dumped, and report dump to nearest battalion headquarters, who should arrange proportionate distribution.

MATERIAL.

Each battalion should have a light German Machine Gun for instruction of Lewis Gunners.

STRAGGLERS POSTS.

Stragglers Posts should be futher forward, and a patrol of mounted police on duty about our original front line.

Infantry belonging to units taking part in the operations should not be used for escorting prisoners back to cages.

RECOMMENDATIONS.

Although a list of recommendations is being submitted I should like to call special attention to the excellent work of the following officers:-

    Lieutenant IDRIS.
    2nd.Lieut. NIGHTINGALE.
      "   LEAPMAN.
      "   SMITH.

15/8/18.

C.B. BENSON
Lieut-Col.
Comdg. 6th. Bn. London. Regiment.

SECRET.   6th. Bn. London Regiment.   Copy. No.
                                                              21/8/18.
                    Operation Order No. 5.

Map 62 D.

1. The Battalion will move to neighbourhood of NEILLY tomorrow.

2. Starting Point -   track outside Battalion H.Q. opposite sentries
                       post.

3. Order of March -   A, B, C, D, H.Q.

4. Dress   -   Battle Order with entrenching tool carries in
                       front.

5. Trench stores will carried.

6. Battalion will march by Companies with 200 yards distance between
   Companies.

7. Leading Company will pass starting point at 5.55a.m.

8. Limbers containing Lewis Guns and S.A.A. of each Company will
   follow immediately in rear of that Company. Cookers, Water carts
   Mess cart, Maltise cart and tool limber will be ready to move
   immediately the Battalion moves and will maintain 200 yards
   distance from rear Company. Water carts will be filled and
   instructions given by Adjutant to Sgt. Buckland complied with.

9. Officers kits and any Mess boxes etc etc not required will be
   dumped at Q.M. stores by 5.30a.m.

10. T.O. will detail 1 limber to bring up 4 tents. These will struck
    from amongst those in camp under orders of R.S.M. and should be
    cutched.
    The tents will be returned to this camp on completion of tour.

11. Battle surplus and all details will remain in possession of present
    camp and will be responsible for safe custody and all stores etc
    left behind.
                    REVEILLE   4.15a.m.

12. Tea will be issued at 5a.m. Breakfast will be served on arrival
                    at destination
13. Camp will be left clean and tidy.

14. Acknowledge.

                                                    Capt. & Adjt.

app V

NARRATIVE OF OPERATIONS
on the
26th, 27th, and 28th August 1918.

Reference Map
62.D N.E. & 62.C N.W.

1. On the 25th August the battalion moved at 8.30 a.m. from trenches E. of MORLANCOURT by route march to L.2.a.5.0 reaching this spot about 11 a.m. The battalion was in Brigade Reserve (the 7th and 8th Battalions being in front) and halted in artillery formation on a two company frontage across the road facing E.

The strength of the battalion was 17 Officers and 558 other ranks.

2. At about 5 p.m. I was warned personally by the Brigade Major that the Brigade would move forward that evening to attack the enemy, the objective being a line running E of BILLON WOOD. Lieut-Colonel Johnston M.C. was placed in command of the operation, and from him I received orders to assemble at 7 p.m. in L.4.a and to move forward in artillery formation of lines of platoons on a two company frontage to the trench running from L.5.d.2.0 to L.5.d.3.8.

The 7th.Battalion was to attack in the front line, the 6th.Battalion being in support on the right and the 8th.Battalion on the left. It was then 6.30 p.m. and I informed Col. Johnston that as my battalion was still about 1500 yards in rear of the other two and I still had my instructions to issue, I could not assemble by the hour named. He instructed me to do so as soon as possible, move forward to the trench indicated, and report to him at TRIGGER COPSE. A section of Machine Guns was attached to me. The battalion assembled at 7.30 p.m. and seeing nothing of the other two battalions I moved forward and halted the battalion on the trench being in touch with the Australians on the right, but being unable to find the 8th.Battalion which should have been on my left or the 7th.Battalion in front. The night was dark and wet, and it was not until 11 p.m. that I found Colonel Johnston. I got the battalion into trenches and cover from shell fire which was severe. I was informed by Colonel Johnston that the attack was postponed for that night.

3. OPERATION OF 26th.AUGUST.

About midnight 25/26th.August Colonel Johnston informed me that the attack would take place next morning, the scheme being altered. The 7th.Battalion were to attack on the right, the 8th.Battalion on the left, and the 6th.Battalion were placed in Brigade Support. I spoke to the Brigade Major on the telephone, and he instructed me to keep in close touch with the two front battalions and conform to their movements if they advanced.

4. ZERO hour was at 4.35 a.m. At 6 a.m. being informed that the 7th and 8th Battalions had advanced I moved my battalion into the Ravine at TRIGGER WOOD in L.6.a. During the night I had been subjected to heavy shelling and had lost about 40 other ranks killed and wounded.

5. I remained in the Ravine during the day of the 26th, two companies being posted in a trench on the forward crest of the ravine and the remainder of the battalion resting.

/6. OPERATION of

6. OPERATION OF 27th AUGUST.

At 6.30 p.m. 26th I attended a conference of Commanding Officers at Brigade Headquarters and received particulars of a plan of attack to take place on the following day, the 27th. The battalion was to assemble on a two company frontage on a line running S through COPSE "C" in H.21.d, in two lines. The 1st line had for its objective a line running from A.23.a,7.6 to A.23.c.6.8. The 2nd line was to leap frog and advance to an objective along a line from A.24.a.4.8 to A.24.c.2.6. The distance of the first objective was roughly 1500 yards and of the 2nd objective 2000 yards from the assembly position. The 7th.Battalion were to advance on our right and the 173rd.Brigade on our left. A section of Machine Guns was attached to me. I was to consider myself as under the orders of Lieut-Colonel Johnston, the senior officer in the line.

7. ZERO hour was at 4.55 a.m. on 27th.August, and the battalion commenced to move forward to the assembly at midnight 26/27th. The first line consisted of "A" Company on the right, "C" Company on the left, and the second line of "D" Company on the right and "B" Company on the left. Each company was organised on a two platoon frontage in lines of sections in file, the two front companies having a line of scouts across their front. The strength of the battalion was 17 officers (including 3 at H.Q. and the Medical Officer) and about 450 other ranks.

8. Considerable difficulty was experienced in finding the correct assembly position, but the battalion went forward at Zero hour in good order. At 8 a.m. as I was moving out to reconnoitre and organise the line, I met messages from Os.C. "A" & "B" Companies respectively, stating that they had each reached their objectives.

9. I proceeded to go forward, and at about 9.30 a.m. reached S.Street at approx: A.22.d.0.6. Here I met a lot of men of the battalion, and also of the 7th and 8th battalions, and Capt.Burt-Smith, O.C."A" Coy (who was wounded but carrying on) and Lieut.Whitworth O.C."B" Coy. I pointed out to them that the line they were on was very far short of the 1st. objective, and that we must get forward at once. Captain Burt-Smith, who had been to reconnoitre, stated that he thought the trenches in front were unoccupied.
SOUTH STREET was full of men of the 6th, 7th, and 8th Battns, and of the 173rd.Brigade. I proceeded to endeavour to re-organise, sending all men of the 173rd.Brigade N across the PERONNE ROAD, and endeavouring to sort out the remainder of the men into battalions.
I instructed Lieut.Whitworth to move forward via NORTH AVENUE with a force of about 30 men of the 6th.London Regt, and occupy the trench from A.23.a.3.8 to A.23.a.5.1. This he did without opposition. I then went forward with about 30 men of the 6th.Battn and reconnoitred the trenches from in A.23.c. I found them empty and occupied BLACK STREET to a point 300 yards S of the road. Simultaneously Capt. Jackson of 7th.Battn. under my orders, moved forward and occupied the front line trench between MORTAR ST & MARKET STREET. subsequently extending to the South and getting in touch with the Australians

10. The 1st objective of the battalion was thus gained. I carefully considered the possibility of moving forward, but decided that this was impossible, in view of the very heavy shell fire and machine gun fire to which the trenches were subjected.

11. I then proceeded to the QUARRY at A.28.a.9.3 and reported to Col. Johnston, also establishing my own H.Q. there.

12. At 3 p.m. I returned to BLACK STREET and re-organised my battalion into companies. I found the number to be roughly 200 O.R. I estimated the casualties including stragglers at other ranks.

NARRATIVE OF OPERATION
of the
31st. August 1918.

Reference Map.
62.C-N.W.

1. On the 30th.instant the battalion embussed at 6.30 p.m. on the PERONNE ROAD at a point S.W. of MARICOURT, debussing at 8.30 p.m. at HEM WOOD H.3.a.3.8. It then proceeded by march route to B.23.d, resting in artillery formation in the valley N of JUNCTION WOOD.

2. At 10.30 p.m. I attended at Brigade Headquarters and was informed that certain orders we had received, to act as Van Guard to the Brigade, were cancelled, and I was handed orders for an attack the next morning at 5.10 a.m. on MARRIERES WOOD.

3. The 175th.Brigade was stated to be holding a line running N. & S. approximately through B.18.Central and B.24.Central. The 174th.Brigade was to assemble in their rear, go forward under a barrage through MARRIERES WOOD and consolidate on a line from C.14.c.0.0 to C.19.d.2.4. This line was to be held by Lewis Gun posts only, and the main line of defence was to be on the reverse slope of the Plateau 500 yards in rear. The barrage opened 100 yards in front of the line held by 175th.Brigade, dwelling on that for 20 minutes, and then advancing at the rate of 100 yards every 6 minutes. On reaching the E side of the wood it was to move forward 300 yards.

4. The battalion assembled with great difficulty the night being dark and the country unknown, with no prominent natural features, but was in position by 4.30 a.m. in the usual formation on a frontage of two companies, "C" Company under 2/Lieut.Moore on the right, "D" Coy under Lieut. . .Ball on the left. The 2nd.line consisted of "A" Company under Capt.S.T.Cooke on the right, "B" Company under 2/Lieut.Soulsby on the left. The remaining officers were 2/Lieut.Mason and Foodhams who had joined on the previous day, and 3 officers lent by the 7th.Battn. London Regiment - 2/Lieuts.Harbutt, Butler & Stocken. There were only 7 sergeants. The battalion numbered 344 O.Rs, including 53 on H.Q. No signs could be seen of the 8th.Battalion which should have been on our left, but the 7th.Battalion assembled in our rear in support.

5. Zero hour was at 5.10 a.m. and at that hour the barrage opened. The line advanced in good order at 5.30 a.m. The enemy immediately opened a very heavy counter barrage, but except for this the WOOD was reached with little opposition. The enemy made no attempt to hold the actual wood, but retired to a line 300 yards E of it on the plateau, from which he opened heavy M.G. fire.

6. From this point Australians could be seen advancing along the ridge S of ROAD WOOD, while enemy Machine Guns were still firing on our men from WARY ALLEY TRENCH in C.25.a & b. Captain Cooke took charge of the situation and sent a party of 20 men under C.S.M.Templar S through the wood to attack this trench. The enemy then for the most part surrendered, a few retiring N.E. along the trench towards BOUCHAVESNES. Captain Cooke was thus enabled to clear the plateau, and he then advanced across the valley with a mixed party of the 6th and 8th. battalions, occupying the trench up to C.20.c.6.5 and getting in touch with the Australians on his right.

/7. The Australians

7. The Australians were meeting with strong opposition higher on the ridge, and at their request Captain Cooke detailed a party of 20 men and one Lewis Gun to assist them.
The line was then advanced to the OLD QUARRY at C.20.b.2.2, the Australians forming a line on our right E of and parallel with the BOUCHAVESNES - PERONNE ROAD.

8. A strong post of the 6th, 7th & 8th Battalions was established in the OLD QUARRY and this line was held until the 173rd. Brigade went through on the morning of the 1st. September.

9. The casualties were 1 officer and 11 O.R. Killed and 3 officers and 73 O.R. Wounded and missing.

4/9/18.

Major,
Comdg., 6th. Bn. London Regiment.

-3-

One officer had been killed and 8 wounded, the only officers left, excluding H.Q.Officers, being Lieut.Whitworth, 2/Lieut. Willcocks and 2/Lieut.Trimm.

13. OPERATIONS OF 28th.AUGUST.

At 8 p.m. on the 27th. Colonel Johnston sent for me and informed me that the attack would be continued the following morning, 28th, Zero hour being at 4.55 a.m. I accordingly issued my orders and held a conference of Os.C.Coys at 11.30 p.m.

14. The battalion assembled astride the PERONNE ROAD the centre of the front line being at A.23.a.6.2 and of the 2nd. line at A.23.a.4.2. The objective was the trenches A.24.a.4.7 to A.24.c.1.9 with orders to push out one company to a point at A.19.c.0.4 to form a line of exploitation.
The battalion was organised as follows :-

1st.line "A" Coy on Right   -   "B" Coy on Left.
2nd.line "C" "   "   "   -   "D" "   "   "
The section of machine guns remained attached to me.

15. At Zero hour the battalion moved forward in good order, and the objective was reached without very serious opposition or heavy casualties.

16. At 7 a.m. I reached the front line, and found one officer only was left, viz Lieut.Willcocks, with 2nd.Lieut.Dixon of the M.Gs who had two sections and guns only left. Lieut.Willcocks was severely wounded at about 8 a.m. leaving me with no officer until about 1 p.m. when Lieut.Trimm joined me from the Right with about 30 men.

17. I proceeded at once to organise the defences of the trench, and to consider the possibility of reaching the line of exploitation. The trench was being submitted to heavy artillery and machine gun fire from the left flank and immediate front. I got into touch with the 8th.Battn on the right and 173rd.Brigade on the left.

18. During the morning I succeeded in driving out the M.G.s (2 or 3) to the front of my trench and establishing a post of 8 men at A.24.b.8.2 (approx). I however considered this post untenable, the communication trench and left flank being submitted to very heavy machine gun fire from the N, while the BOSCHE was bombing along the trench from the S. Also I observed about 200 Bosche advancing in artillery formation over the crest at B.19.a.& 6, and fired at them with a Lewis Gun, scattering them. I therefore withdrew the post to the main line of defence. The sector remained quiet during the remainder of the day, except for heavy and continuous shelling and M.G. fire. These appeared to die away towards the evening and finally ceased about 10.0 p.m.

19. At 8 p.m. on the 28th I was ordered to establish a strong post under an officer as far forward as possible at A.24.d.3.0, the advance being covered by artillery, particulars of which would be furnished to me. I received no details, but at 10.15 p.m. the fire became very heavy. I therefore sent the party forward at 10.30 p.m. under 2/Lieut.Woodhams and the post was formed at A.24.d.3.0 without opposition, no sign being seen of the Bosche. 2nd Lt Woodhams was one of 3 new officers who had been posted to me on the previous evening

20. During the night the Battalion was relieved by the 12th.Bn.London Regiment, and retired into reserve at

21. The casualties from 23-28th inclusive were 1 officer and 29 OR killed and 9 officers and 191 OR wounded and missing

Major,

WAR DIARY
or
INTELLIGENCE SUMMARY.

(Erase heading not required.)

Army Form C. 2118.

6 London R

Vol 21

Place	Date	Hour	Summary of Events and Information	Remarks and references to Appendices
Sept 1916	1		Battⁿ holding line in front of HARRIER'S WOOD. H.Q. at B.2.d.3.5.	ac
	2	5pm	Important line move forward to HINDLEG WOOD. Battⁿ relieved by 4th Div. and moved back by trench route to bivouac in B.20.d.	ac
	3		Battⁿ resting and refitting	ac
	4		Ditto. Reorganising and training (Close order drill, musketry, bayonet attacks)	ac
	5		Ditto	ac
	6		Battⁿ spent day burying and carrying work to twenty sap in D.4.d and D.6.d. H.Q. at D.8.c.70. Battⁿ on Bus to HARICOURT (Plumbin Ridge North)	ac
	7	11am	Battⁿ moved by march route to GUYENCOURT in support of attack by yth London. Transport bivouacs moved to POISLAINS.	ac
	8	3.30pm	Battⁿ moved to front of assembly in E.3.b.4.th H.Q. at E.3.b.4.51.	ac
	9	9pm	Battⁿ relieved yth London in front line in sunken road in E.12.c. H.Q. at E.6.A.22. Battⁿ Gallantry taking Leuzo Wood F.K.C.	ac

WAR DIARY
or
INTELLIGENCE SUMMARY.
(Erase heading not required.)

Army Form C. 2118.

Place	Date	Hour	Summary of Events and Information	Remarks and references to Appendices
[illegible]	10	3.0 A.M	3rd London assembled behind our front line to pass through and continue our attack at dawn. 3rd London attacked but forced to withdraw owing to heavy M.G. fire, then held front line in conjunction with the Battⁿ. Battⁿ. relieved by 4th Suffolks and marched back by march route to LIERAMONT.	Ap⁹
		11 A.M	Total casualties during period 8/10th.— OFFICERS.— 2 wounded. MAJOR J. VENNING. 2/Lt A.C. LASHAM O.R.s killed 8. wounded 41. Missing 23. Both 2nd in rear and the Major R.B. VINCE D.S.O M.C founded and assumed command of the Battⁿ.	Ap⁹
	11			Ap⁹
	12		Battⁿ. moved by march route to GUYENCOURT. Wearing 3 hrs later O.R⁰ or E.B.C.I.S Follow⁹ Officers joined for duty.— 2/Lts. E.A. BOWERS-TAYLOR. A.M.H. BULL. C.A. FULLER. J. ROSS. G.H. PARTRIDGE. A.J. YEO. D.F. BRADSTREET. D. FROST. P. MACGREGOR. F.T. RAEMERS. W.S. STOLL.	Ap⁹

Army Form C. 2118.

WAR DIARY
or
INTELLIGENCE SUMMARY.
(Erase heading not required.)

Place	Date	Hour	Summary of Events and Information	Remarks and references to Appendices
Sept 1916	13		Battⁿ arrived GUYEN COURT.	
	14		Capt. and Adj^t. R. WYLIE M.G. to Hospital (sick)	
			2/Lt. H.V. STOCKEN " "	
			2/Lt. S.J. BUTLER. Adjourned 7th London	
			Capt. S.T. COOKE assumed temporary duties of Adjutant.	
			Battⁿ moved forward and relieved 9th London in sunken road running	
			N.28.C – E.4.B.48. 9/R at N.28.C.9.4	
	15	Mid^{nt}	Battⁿ relieved by 2/1st London and moved back by march route to bivouacs	
			in WILLE WOOD. H.Q at E.9.c.3.6.	
	16		Battⁿ resting and re-fitting	
	17		Reorganizing and refitting – Platoons in attack – Ditto	
	18		" Ditto "	
	19		" Ditto "	
	20		" Ditto " 2/Lt C.F. MASON to Hospital (sick)	

WAR DIARY or INTELLIGENCE SUMMARY.

Army Form C. 2118.

(Erase heading not required.)

Place	Date	Hour	Summary of Events and Information	Remarks and references to Appendices
Sept 1918	20.		Following Honours published in IIInd Corps. Routine Orders dated 16/9/18:-	
			Lt Col. C.B. BENSON. D.S.O. — Bar to D.S.O.	
			Lt (A/Capt. E.L.) HANIDRIS — M.C.	
			2/Lt. L.C. LEAPMAN — M.C.	
			2/Lt. H.G.C. NIGHTINGALE — M.C.	
			2/Lt. A.E.S. SMITH — M.C.	
	21.	9 A.M.	Battn moved by march route to LIERAMONT. H.Q. at E.4.c.2.9.	
		8 P.M.	Battn moved by march route to RAILWAY EMBANKMENT in E.23.A.40. H.Q. at E.23.A.7.2.	
			MAJOR. N.B. VINCE. D.S.O. M.C. relinquished command of the Battalion	
			CAPT. S.T. COOKE assumed command of the Battalion.	
	22.	4 P.M.	Battn moved by march route to RONSSOY and area. A and C Coys in trenches from F.16.C.75 to F.22.A.13. B and D Coys in RONSSOY.	

Army Form C. 2118.

WAR DIARY
or
INTELLIGENCE SUMMARY.
(Erase heading not required.)

Instructions regarding War Diaries and Intelligence Summaries are contained in F. S. Regs., Part II. and the Staff Manual respectively. Title pages will be prepared in manuscript.

Place	Date	Hour	Summary of Events and Information	Remarks and references to Appendices
Sept 1916	22	(noon M)	Relieving 4th BUFFS. (14th Div.) H.Q. at F.21.b.7.3.	M/c
	23		2/Lt H.D. DUFF joined for duty.	M/c
			Batt⁰ holding GREEN LINE around ROMSSOY as above.	M/c
	24		Batt⁰ relieved by III/105th American Regt and moved back by march route to VILLERS FAUCON. Hence by busses to HEILLY arriving there 9 a.m.	M/c
	25		Batt⁰ in billets around HEILLY. 2/Lt C.B. BENSON D.S.O. rejoined from leave. 2/Lt L.C. LEAPHAM MC. Hospital.	M/c
R/Sheet [ENS II.	26	noon	Batt⁰ moved by train from HEILLY to SAVY (Operation Orders No.134)	M/c
		4 p.m.	Batt⁰ debussed at SAVY and moved by march route to billets around CHATEAU DE L'HAUTE	
	27		Batt⁰ resting and refitting.	M/c

Army Form C. 2118.

WAR DIARY
or
INTELLIGENCE SUMMARY.
(Erase heading not required.)

Place	Date	Hour	Summary of Events and Information	Remarks and references to Appendices
S.K.11/48	28		Battⁿ reorganizing training etc.	ML
	29.		MAJOR S.J.M. SAMPSON. M.C. joined for duty. Bay. Church Service. 2Lt. D. FROST to Hospital (sick) Lt.Col. C.B. BENSON. D.S.O. temporarily in command of 17th Infantry Brigade	ML
	30.		MAJOR S.J.M. SAMPSON. M.C. assumed temporary command of the Battalion. Bat.H.Q^{rs} moved by march route to LES BREBIS (Sheet 36cN.W. No.125)	ML

SECRET.

OPERATION ORDER NO. 165
6th BN., LONDON REGT.

Copy No....
6/9/16

Reference Map - 62D, N.W.

1. The battalion will move this afternoon by bus and march route.

2. Starting Point. Track opposite Orderly Room.

3. Order of March - A, B, C, D & H.Q. Attached to H.Q. will be N.C.Os. for return to England.

4. Dress: Battle Order.

5. Battle Surplus will not parade with Battalion.

6. Distance of 200 yards will be maintained between Companies.

7. Leading platoon will pass starting point at 7.0 p.m.

8. Route: Point on HEM - MAUREPAS Road at B.27.a.0.1, where busses will be met.

9. Battalion will embus after 7th Bn. have embussed.

10. 2/Lieut. Hodges will meet Staff Captain at embussing point at 5.45 p.m. and will take with him embussing state.

11. C.Q.M. Sgts. and Storemen will march and embus with H.Q.

12. Officers kits, mess-boxes, orderly room boxes will be dumped outside Orderly Room by 5 p.m.

13. Tents and bivvies will be struck, tightly rolled and stacked at same place by 4.30 p.m.

14. R.S.M. has already been detailed to leave guard.

15. Dry rations for tomorrows consumption will be issued before departure. Meat ration will be carried and cooked on cookers.

16. All water bottles will be filled by 5 p.m. at latest.

17. Battle Surplus will parade under 2/Lieut. Maple at a place and time to be notified later.

18. Separate instructions will be issued to T.O.

19. All details other than transport and cooks will parade with H.Q. The C.S.M. of H.Q. will take steps to obtain correct embussing state.

20. Embussing state from Coys. and H.Q. will be handed in to Orderly Room by 5 p.m.

21. Any O.R. arriving today from leave, guards, etc. will have S.A.A. made up to 170 rounds per man. This if necessary will be taken from Battle Surplus.

22. 4 Lewis Guns and 16 magazines per gun will be carried.

23. All trench stores etc. will be carried.

24. All company flags, notice boards, etc. etc., will be carefully packed and stacked outside Orderly Room by 4.30 p.m.

25. Acknowledge.

(Sgd) R. WYLIE, Capt. & Adjt.

SUMMARY of OPERATIONS

September 8th, 9th, 10th 1918.

Ref.
Map Sheet 62C N.E.

The Battalion assembled at 3.30 a.m. in E3, b and d. in support of the attack being made by 7th and 8th Battalions.

At 5 a.m. B Company (under Capt. Idris, M.C.) went forward to establish liaison with the 74th Division on the right, to establish a liaison post at KNOLL POST if and when reached, and subsequently to fill in the gap which would occur between the two divisions during a further advance.

This Company then went over behind the 7th Battalion, and a few hours after zero found that this Battalion had been held up, and that it had passed through the 7th Battalion. It therefore consolidated its position in a sunken road S.W. of EPEHY. Later it was reinforced by small parties from the 7th Battalion.

At 3 p.m. on receipt of instructions from Brigade, A Company were ordered to attack Machine Gun nests in E.12.d from the rear, taking a route via VILLERS FAUCON. This operation was afterwards cancelled.

C and D Companies remained in Brigade support in E.3.b until dusk, when the 6th Battalion relieved 7th Battalion in the front line (Night 8/9th).

On completion of the relief B and D Companies immediately pushed on, and established our front line in the sunken road E.12.c, S.W. of EPEHY, C Company being in support and A Company in reserve, Battalion Headquarters being established at E.5.d.2.2. The Battalion was supported by a Section of B Company, 58th M.G.Bn.

9th. At 5.30 a.m. D Company (under Lieut. N.S. Kidson, M.C.) went forward to occupy EPEHY which was believed to be evacuated. It was met by strong resistance and heavy M.G. fire and forced to withdraw to its own lines.

During the morning touch was established with 74th Division on the right. The left flank was in the air but was covered as far as possible by the M.G. Section in the rear.

Night 8/9th. C Company under 2/Lieut. Moore was sent forward under the orders of the Commanding Officer (Major Venning) to reinforce the Companies in the front line.

9th: These three Companies continued to hold the line during the day, but it was found necessary to clear the ground N. and E. of our front line during the night to prepare for the attack by the 173rd Brigade.

At 11.55 p.m. C Company therefore went forward North of the front line (sunken road in E.12.c) and B Company to the East, searching and clearing the ground of enemy outposts. This was done with little resistance.

At 5.15 a.m. on 10th, 173rd Brigade made an unsuccessful attempt to occupy EPEHY and the remnants fell back upon our

Sheet 2.

position.

During the afternoon the Commanding Officer of the 3rd Battalion with 8 of his own men and 1 officer and 16 men of the 6th Battalion cleared the trenches North of our position and South of EPEHY. These trenches were subsequently occupied by 6th Battalion and a few men of 3rd Battalion.

At night the Battalion was relieved by 1/4th Suffolks, and went into billets at LIERAMONT.

(Sgd)   R. WYLIE.

Capt. & Adt.,
6th Bn., London Regiment.

11th September 1918.

SECRET. OPERATION ORDER No. 124
6th BN., LONDON REGIMENT.   25-9-18
Ref. Map Sheets   Copy No.....
AMIENS 1.
LENS 11.   Reveille -   6.0 a.m.
                 Breakfast -   7.0 a.m.

1.   The Battalion will move to SAVY BERLETTE tomorrow 26th
instant.   Entraining Station - HEILLY.

2.   All Officers' valises, mess-boxes, medical stores, signal
stores, and orderly-room boxes will be dumped at Quartermaster's
Stores at 8.30 a.m.

3.   All Lewis Guns, Magazines, and Spare Parts Bags to be loaded
on limbers under the supervision of Sgt. Royston by 8.30 a.m.

4.   All water-bottles to be filled by 8.30 a.m.

5.   O.C., A, B, and C Companies will each detail one officer
and 40 men, and O.C. D Company one officer and 30 men, to report in
full marching order at HEILLY Station at 8.0 a.m. This party
will parade outside Bn.H.Q. at 7.30 a.m. and will be marched to the
Station under the senior officer present, and will proceed by the
first train leaving HEILLY 9.30 a.m. This party will act as
unloading party to the Brigade group at detraining station and will
report on arrival at same to Brigade detraining officer, Capt.
A.J.C. Lintott, M.C. The officer in charge of this party will
detail one officer to act as detraining officer who will report to
Capt. Lintott as above.

6.   The Battalion will parade in full marching order, with
soft caps, in column of route facing the Church, at 11 a.m. in
the following order:
                Headquarters
                A Company
                B   "
                C   "
                D   "
Head of Column outside Bn.H.Q.

7.   2/Lt. A.J. Yeo will act as entraining officer of the 6th
Bn., London Regiment, and will report to the Brigade entraining
officer at HEILLY station at 9.0 a.m. He will supervise the
entrainment of personnel of the Battalion. This Officer will
report at Bn.H.Q. at 8.30 a.m. for the entraining states of the
personnel and transport of the Battalion - these he will hand to
the Brigade entraining officer on arrival at the Station.

8.   All transport will be loaded and ready to move at 9.15 a.m.
Transport to arrive at Station at 9.55 a.m.

9.   Company Commanders will inform their men of standing
orders re discipline whilst travelling by rail, and on no occasion
will any man leave the train whilst en route without the permission
of an officer.
        March discipline will be strictly maintained during the march
to the entraining station and from the detraining station.

10.   All billets will be left in a clean and tidy condition and
a report to this effect will be rendered to the Bn. Orderly Room
by 10.30 a.m.

11.   ACKNOWLEDGE.

                                         S.T. COOKE,
Distribution - See over.   Capt. & A/Adjt.

Distribution:

        No. 1. Commanding Officer.
            2. O.C., A Company.
            3.   "   B   "
            4.   "   C   "
            5.   "   D   "
            6. O i/c. H.Q. and Medical Officer.
            7. Quartermaster and Transport Officer.
            8. R.S.M. and Sgt. Royston.
         9/10. War Diary.
           11. File.

        Issued at 11.30 p.m.

SECRET   OPERATION ORDER   No. 195.

                    4th Bn., LONDON REGIMENT.
                                                          Copy No. 10
Ref. Map Sheet   Date .29-9-18..
44A - 1/40000.
LENS 11. - 1/100000.   Reveille -   5.30 a.m.
                        Breakfast -   7.0 a.m.
                        Dinner on Arrival.
                        Tea -   5.0 p.m.

1.   The Battalion will move from present location by march route
to Les Brebis tomorrow, the 30th September 1918.

2.   Order of March:

                    Headquarters
                    A Company
                    B   "
                    C   "
                    D   "

        Starting Point will be the ~~blockhouse~~ CHATEAU GATES on the VILLERS
AU BOIS - MARET HERVIEU Road.
        The leading Company will pass Starting Point at 9-15 a.m.
        200 yards distance will be maintained between Companies. Companies
in rear must keep connection with Companies in front.

3.   ROUTE: CHATEAU GATES - WOOD CROSS ROADS above first "R" in
MAISNIL-BOUCHE - GOUY SERVINS - MON DE BOUVIGNY - BOUVIGNY - AIX
NOULETTE - BULLY GRENAY - LES BREBIS.

4.   DRESS: Full Marching Order, Soft Caps will be worn.
Water bottles filled.

5.   Lewis Guns, Ammunition, Spare Parts Bags, will be loaded
under the supervision of Sgt. Goodall by 8.30 a.m. at the Transport
lines.
        Officers valises, mess-boxes, Signal Stores, Medical Stores,
Orderly Room boxes, and etc., will be dumped at Q.M.'s Stores by
8.45 a.m.

6.   The Camp will be left in a spotless condition and Companies
will render a certificate that this has been done to Battalion
Orderly Room by 8.30 a.m.
        Special attention is to be paid to the following:-
Mess-kitchens, Officers' kitchens, Tables, Shelves, Space
underneath huts, Incinerators, Latrines, Grease Traps, Ablution
tables. Fire buckets are to be refilled with clean water.
        One officer and one platoon of D Company will remain behind
as Rear-party under the Orders of 2/Lt. G.U.L.Tubb, who will obtain
from the District Commandant a certificate to the effect that the
Camp has been left in a clean and sanitary condition.

7.   Marching out states are to be rendered to Battalion Orderly
Room by 8.30 a.m.
        Marching in states to be forwarded within one hour of arrival
at destination.
        O.C., D Company, will show rear party separately on both
states. Differences between (a) Daily numbers in Camp, (b) Marching
out states, and (c) Marching in states must be explained.

Sheet 2.

8. Guns and Ammunition will be drawn immediately on arrival.

9. Company Cookers will follow Companies with fires alight ready to serve dinner on arrival.

10. Transport will follow in rear of Battalion leaving Camp at 10 a.m.

S.T. COOKE.
Capt. & A/Adjt.
4th Bn., London Regt.

Distribution:
No. 1. Commanding Officer.
2. O.C., A Coy.
3. "   B "
4. "   C "
5. "   D "
6. "   H.Q., and Medical Officer.
7. QM. and T.O.
8. (R.S.M. and Sgt. Goodall.
   (Sgt. Walter Cook.
9/10. War Diary.
11. File.

Issued at ....20-9-18.

Maps: Sheet 44a (36c) S.W. 26
Sh.9 44a

Army Form C. 2118.

WAR DIARY
INTELLIGENCE SUMMARY
(Erase heading not required.)

Place	Date	Hour	Summary of Events and Information	Remarks and references to Appendices
	October 1918			
LE BREBIS.	1.		Battalion accommodated in billets – Spent Training	
LENS N.W.	2.		Moved to support position N.W. of LENS with Bn HQ at Harrow's Gates. Transport lines & Am Stores Battle Surplus to Divl Reception Camp. Capt H.L. JOHNSTON remained at LE BREBIS.	
			rejoined from Hospital. 9 of H.S. OR joined for duty	
	4.		Relieved 8th Bn London Regt in right subsector of Brigade front with two companies in line and two in support.	
	5.		1 OR wounded. 1 OR wounded at duty.	
	7.		10 OR reinforcements joined.	
	8.		11 OR reinforcements joined.	
BOIS DE RIAUMONT	8/9.		Relieved by 12th Bn London Regt and proceeded to find reserve in locality of BOIS DE RIAUMONT with Bn HQ at M.29.c.25.65. Bn accommodated in cellar billets. Transport lines and Qm Stores remained at LE BREBIS.	
	9/12.		Cleaning up, refitting and training	
	11.		9 OR reinforcements joined	
CANAL DE LA HAUTE.	12.		Bn moved by march route from BOIS DE RIAUMONT and took up outpost line W. of CANAL DE LA HAUTE with Bn HQ at Q.18.c.5.5. Reconnoitring patrols were	

Army Form C. 2118.

WAR DIARY
INTELLIGENCE SUMMARY.
(Erase heading not required.)

Page 2.

Instructions regarding War Diaries and Intelligence Summaries are contained in F. S. Regs., Part II. and the Staff Manual respectively. Title pages will be prepared in manuscript.

Place	Date	Hour	Summary of Events and Information	Remarks and references to Appendices
	October 1918			
CANAL DE LA HAUTE	12.		Patrols continually sent out to maintain touch with the enemy. Spt Lines and Am Stores moved from LE BREBIS to CITIE ST PIERRE. 10 OR reinforcements joined.	
	13.		Bn HQ moved from O.18.c.5.5. to O.5.a.b.4. owing to lack of wire with which to obtain telephonic communication with Bde HQ. Wiring patrolling took place and touch maintained. Casualties:- 1 OR killed. 1 OR wounded.	
	14.		Enemy in strength of approximately 50 OR raided post in P.1. d.4.5. After inflicting casualties the enemy took prisoner the remainder and then withdrew. Casualties:- 2nd Lt. W.E. BRADSTREET wounded. 10 OR killed. 14 OR wounded. 8 OR missing believed killed. Bn HQ moved from O.5.a.b.4 to O.18.e.S.5. on telephonic communication being established. Bn ordered to cross the canal and establish bridgeheads but owing to resistance was unable to do so. Spt lines and Am Stores moved from CITIE ST PIERRE to MONTIGNY. 4 OR reinforcements joined.	
COURRIERES	15		Relieved in line by 9th Bn. London Regt and moved into Bell Reserve at COURRIERES arriving accommodation in billets. Bn HQ at O.5.b.3.8.	
	16.		Cleaning up, refitting, etc. Lieut (A/Capt) E.G. GODFREY. M.C. joined and assumed	

Army Form C. 2118.

WAR DIARY
INTELLIGENCE SUMMARY.
(Erase heading not required.)

Page 3.

Place	Date	Hour	Summary of Events and Information	Remarks and references to Appendices
COURRIERES	October 1918 16		duties of Acting Adjutant	
	17		Bn moved forward and established staff on E. edge of CANAL DE LA HAUTE position. Billets being as cleared enemy riding school in BOIS DES HAUTOIS. V.32.a.	
	17	1500	Bn moved forward to OIGNES and accommodated in billets. 7 OR reinforcements joined. Opt line from MONTIGNY to COURRIERES and from COURRIERES to OIGNES.	J.E. End pays
	18	0300	Bn moved to outskirts of MONS EN PEVELE at which time it became Brigade support. 8th Bn London Regt then holding outpost line approx E. edge of BERSEE. During the moving a line in support of 8th Bn London Regt was formed along that general lines L.14.a. and c and L.20.a. and c and L.13.d. L.19.b and d and opt lines occupied by A and B companies in front. Bn HQ at L.24.d. 25.95. and Bn Stores from OIGNES to VINCOURT	J.E. Coffey
	19		Bn passed through outposts of 8th Bn and became advanced guard to 174 Inf Bde. Attached to the unit were :- 1 Section R.F.A. 1 Section L.T.M. By. 1 Coy M.G. Bn when rear guard was fired upon by M. Guns from a house at G.8.a. 20.45. and after this opposition tactics for an hour and was probably made in order to get away some light artillery stationed	J.E. Coffey

WAR DIARY
of
INTELLIGENCE SUMMARY.
(Erase heading not required.)

Army Form C. 2118.

Instructions regarding War Diaries and Intelligence Summaries are contained in F. S. Regs., Part II. and the Staff Manual respectively. Title pages will be prepared in manuscript.

Page 4.

Place	Date	Hour	Summary of Events and Information	Remarks and references to Appendices
	19		near by, the movement of which was distinctly heard. This was corroborated by inhabitants	
			One prisoner taken at G.7.b.8.5. No further opposition was met and the Battalion took	G.G.G.
			up an outpost line in E and outskirts of NOMAIN for the night along the general line -	
			road in B.25.c. H.1.a and d.	
	20		Towards dawn battle patrols established at posts H.2.a.3.7. and B.25.c.8.3.	G.G.G
		0800	3rd Bn. London Regt passed through outpost line and this Bn was withdrawn and billeted in	
			the North portion of NOMAIN, where it became Divisional reserve. for line from	
			VINCOURT to NOMAIN.	
NOMAIN	21.		Resting and cleaning up in vicinity of billets	G.G.G
	22.		Capt. G.G. ROSE-INNES. Lieut. H.W. POTTS. 2nd Lt. J.G. ROBERTSON joined. 5 OR reinforcements	G.G
	23.		Capt. L.B. Tillard joined. 2nd Lt. H.D. DUFF sick to Hospital	G.G.
	24/26		Training in vicinity of billets	G.G.G.
RONGY.	27		Bn. moved by march route to RONGY and accommodated in billets, taking up position of	
			Brigade Reserve. Bn HQ at I.4.b.9.2.	G.G.G
	28.		Routes and approaches in forward area reconnoitered by all officers. Capt. L.B. Tillard	
			reported to BEE HQ on our right as B.E.E. Liaison Officer (36 Bde. 12 Division)	G.G

Army Form C. 2118.

WAR DIARY
or
INTELLIGENCE SUMMARY.
(Erase heading not required.)

Page 5.

Place	Date	Hour	Summary of Events and Information	Remarks and references to Appendices
	October 1915			
RONGY	28/31		Training, smartening up drills carried on in vicinity of billets.	
			2nd Lt. L.C. LEAPMAN from leave.	

V. C. Ashby
Captain and Acting Adjutant
6th Bn. The London Regiment.

WAR DIARY

INTELLIGENCE SUMMARY.

(Erase heading not required.)

Page 1.

Place	Date	Hour	Summary of Events and Information	Remarks and references to Appendices
	November 1918.			
RONGY.	1.		Battalion in support position and accommodated in billets at RONGY with H.Q. at I.4.b.9.2.	C.E.G.
	2/3.		General training carried on in vicinity of billets	C.E.G.
	4.		Training continued in vicinity of billets	C.E.G.
			- do - Lt V.V. BALL rejoined from base. 2nd Lt. L.G. WATSON rejoined from employment at H.Q. 58R Divn.	C.E.G.
	5/7.		- do - 2nd Lt. E.R. COLES joined for duty 6.11.1918.	C.E.G.
BLEHAIRES.	8	1100 hrs	Battalion moved by march route to BLEHAIRES in support position	C.E.G.
		1600 hrs	Battalion moved forward in close support of 2/2nd Bn London Rgt, crossed the L'HAULTE Canal with Bn HQ at CIN.	App. I.
ROCOURT.	9		Moved forward as advance guard to 174 Inf. Bde and rested during night in vicinity of ROCOURT with HQ at F.8.C.4.3. (Sheet 44)	C.E.G.
BELOEIL.	10.		Advance continued today. The Battalion was passed through by 7th Bn London Rgt and proceeded to BELOEIL where it remained for the night.	App II
			2nd Lt. W. STOLL transferred to England sick.	C.E.G.
	11		Advance continued Orders received at 10.00 hrs that armistice was signed and hostilities would cease at 11.00 hrs. At 11.00 hrs the Battalion was in GRUSAGE and remained	C.E.G.

Maps Sheets 44 and 45.   Army Form C. 2118.

WAR DIARY
INTELLIGENCE SUMMARY.

Page 2.

Place	Date	Hour	Summary of Events and Information	Remarks and references to Appendices
	November 1918.			
GROSAGE	11		Stationary there and was accommodated in billets.	C.E.G.
	12/16		2nd Lt. H. DUFF classified B1. by medical board. General training. Education scheme for all ranks organized.	C.E.G.
PERUWELZ	17		Bn. moved by march route to PERUWELZ and accommodated in billets. Bn H.Q. at L.3.a.7.9.	App. III C.E.G.
	18/21		General training and Education Classes. 2nd Lt. E.O. WILLINGHAM joined for duty 21/11/1918.	C.E.G.
	22/24		do Lieut A.V. PLUNKETT M.C. 2nd Lt E.G. MONEY	C.E.G.
	25/28		do 2nd Lt. H.F. WILLCOCKS joined for duty 24/11/1918.	C.E.G.
	29		Inspection of Battalion by Brig. Gen. A. MAXWELL D.S.O comdg 174th Inf Bde.	C.E.G.
	30.		General Training and Education Classes. Strength of Battalion 40 Off 729 O.Ranks. 36 " 683 " Nos present.	C.E.G.

E.V. Godfrey Captain & A/Adjutant
13th Bn. London Regiment.

WAR DIARY
INTELLIGENCE SUMMARY.

6th Inniskilling Regt. Army Form C. 2118.

Vol 26

Place	Date	Hour	Summary of Events and Information	Remarks and references to Appendices
	February 1919			
PERUWELZ	1		General Training & Education	
	2		Church Parade	
	3		General Training & Education	
	4		General Training & Education	
	5		General Training & Education — About Capt B. Field & 2 Lt A.W. Few & 2 Lt R. Humphreys	
	6		General Training & Education	
	7		General Training & Education	
	8		General Training & Education — Battalion Dance at Cinema. Capt H. Johnson	
			w.e.f. 5th Feb. Antedated 5½" Reversion	
	9		Church Parade.	
	10		General Training and Education — Lt Mc Patts and 2nd Lt Humphreys	
			2/Lieut O.R. Cobo reported for duty	
	11		General Training and Education	
	12		General Training & Education	
	13		General Training & Education — 23 O.R. Demobilysed	
	14		General Training & Education — 24 O.R. Demobilysed	

Army Form C. 2118.

WAR DIARY
or
INTELLIGENCE SUMMARY.
(Erase heading not required.)

Place	Date	Hour	Summary of Events and Information	Remarks and references to Appendices
PERUWELZ	15		General training and education - 25 OR demobilized	
	16		Church Parade - 1 OR demobilized	
	17		General Library and education - 2/Lieut. J. Given to leave	
	18		General training and education	
	19		General training and education - 2/Lieut J.S. Manifee joined from 3rd Bn. 2 OR demobilised	
	20		General training and education - 5 OR demobilised. Draft of 85 OR received from London Regt.	
	21		General training, organization and education - Draft of 12 from 2nd Batt. London Regt.	
	22		General training & reorganisation	
	23		General training & reorganisation	
	24		Battalion moved to ROUCOURT by march route. Arrived at 1115 hours. Draft of 4 Off + 24 OR from 8th Bn. London Regt and 5 off + 211 OR from 7th London Regt. 11 Off + 34 men transferred to 7th London Regt for demobilization or repatriation. Lewis gun coys + Sun. Sgts.	

WAR DIARY
INTELLIGENCE SUMMARY
(Erase heading not required.)

Army Form C. 2118.

Place	Date	Hour	Summary of Events and Information	Remarks and references to Appendices
	24 (Cont.d)		Officers joined from 5th Bn. from 7th Bn. Officers transferred to 7th Bn.	
			Major R. CR Woolard M.C. Major R.J. Farrell D.S.O. Major R.B. Bradley	
			" J. Cancellor Capt. Lieut. Coleridge "(Major) R.J. Godfrey M.C.	
			2/Lt. R.B. Pattinson M.C. 2/Lt. R.B. Cookson " J. Bell	
			" J.R. Marchom " 1/4O.D. Maple-Jennes 2/Lt. G.R. Bond	
			" " H. Chandler " D. Fox	
				" Hardinge
				" J.L. Devenay
				" J. Snow
				" A.B. Chambers
				" E.L. Willingham
				" H. Muncey
	25		General Training & organization - Inspection of Public by Divisional Lt. Gen.	
	26		Inspection of Battalion by Brig. General Street. A.M. Hampton Bere to leave	
	27		Inspection of Battalion by Assumed General and farewell address	

WAR DIARY
or
INTELLIGENCE SUMMARY.
(Erase heading not required.)

Army Form C. 2118.

Place	Date	Hour	Summary of Events and Information	Remarks and references to Appendices
ROUVROY.	27/(cont)		2/Lieut P. ASTLEY joined from 1st Battn. 2/Lieut E.A. BAYERS TAYLOR to leave	7/M
	28		2/Lieut W.J. BROWN joined from 3rd Battn. 7/M	
			Battalion moved to LEUZE by two routes and entrained for Germany	7/M
			at approximately 1200 hours. 7/M 2/Lieut H.E. ROWMAN M.C. and 2/Lieut C.A. FRY. 7/M	
			2nd 23 OR to leave	7/M
			Off. OR	
			Strength of Battn. 28 828	7/M
			Number present 22 631	7/M

J. Mumford
Capt. a/Lt Col.
6th Bn. London Regt.

58 DIVISION
174 BDE

2/6 BN LONDON REGT
1915 SEPT — 1916 FEB
1917 JAN — 1918 JAN

ABSORBED BY 1/6 BN 1918 FEB

www.ingramcontent.com/pod-product-compliance
Lightning Source LLC
Chambersburg PA
CBHW081430160426
43193CB00013B/2236